Sound Advance!

Sound Advance!
Experiences of an Officer of H.M. 50th Regt. in Australia, Burma & During the Gwalior War, in India

Joseph Anderson

Including
A Brief History of Anderson's Campaigns
by Eric Sheppard

Sound Advance!: Experiences of an Officer of H.M. 50th Regt. in Australia, Burma & During the Gwalior War, in India
by Joseph Anderson

Including *A Brief History of Anderson's Campaigns*
by Eric Sheppard

First published in 1913 in
Recollections of a Peninsular Veteran

A Brief History of Anderson's Campaigns by Eric Sheppard
has been adapted by the Leonaur editors from
A Short History of the British Army to 1914
first published in 1926

FIRST EDITION

Published by Leonaur Ltd

Material original to this book and the entire text in this form
copyright © 2007 Leonaur Ltd

ISBN: 978-1-84677-150-7 (hardcover)
ISBN: 978-1-84677-142-2 (softcover)

www.leonaur.com

Publisher's Notes

In the interests of authenticity, the spellings, grammar and place names used have been retained from the original editions.

The opinions of the authors represent a view of events in which he was a participant related from his own perspective, as such the text is relevant as an historical document.

The views expressed in this book are not necessarily those of the publisher.

Contents

Introduction	7
Bound for Australia	9
Norfolk Island	14
Sunday Services at Norfolk Island	20
Life at Norfolk Island	26
Mangalore Cattle Station	32
On My Defence	41
Ordered to Calcutta	46
Life at Calcutta	51
At Moulmein	57
Voyage Up the Ganges	62
In Command at Cawnpore	68
The Gwalior War	73
Wounded and Made Much Of	81
Return to Cawnpore	86
On Leave for Two Years	91
Australia Once More	96
Second Voyage to Calcutta	101
To Cawnpore and Back	107
India to Cape Town	112
Return to England	118
Farewell to the 50th Regiment	123
A Brief History of Anderson's Campaigns	127
A Note on the Gwalior War	157

Introduction

The following pages have been selected from the autobiography of my grandfather, the late Colonel Joseph Anderson, who was born in Sutherlandshire, Scotland, on June 1, 1790, and died on July 18, 1877. It should be stated that this narrative was written only for his own family. He had never kept a diary—nor even any notes of his adventures and travels—and only began to write his reminiscences of the long-past years when he was seventy-four, in the quiet of his beautiful home near Melbourne, Australia. His memory was perfectly amazing; but if any slight inaccuracies should be discovered, the reader is asked to excuse them, on account of his age. He was a "grand old man" in every sense, and lived in excellent health of mind and body until his eighty-eighth year. To the very last he was always keenly interested in military matters, and never failed to attend, in uniform, all the important volunteer reviews held in Melbourne, where his upright, soldierly figure attracted universal admiration. His son, the late Colonel Acland Anderson, C.M.G., was for many years the Colonel-Commandant of the Military Forces of H.M. Government in Victoria, which appointment he held till his death in January, 1882. He was the founder of the Volunteer Organization, as in 1855 he raised a Rifle Corps in Melbourne, which was not only the first in Victoria but probably the first in Australia.

Acland Anderson
Captain, late 3rd Dragoon Guards , September, 1913

Chapter 1

Bound for Australia

After my adventures in Egypt and Europe I was to go to New South Wales on the ship *Parmelia,* which took on board some of her freight of convicts at Gravesend, then sailed for the Cove of Cork to embark the remainder; there we received two hundred more, making in all about three hundred criminals. They were under the medical charge of Dr. Donoughoe, a very pleasing Irishman, and our captain during the voyage was equally pleasant.

We were detained some weeks at the Cove from adverse winds and other causes, and during that time it was very distressing to witness the daily scenes which took place between the Irish convicts and their numerous heart-broken relations. They came in boatloads to our ship daily; they were not allowed to come on board, but only to talk to their kindred, who crowded over the ship's side or at the port-holes, and these interviews lasted for hours. At last, about the beginning of November, 1833, we got clear off and sailed for Sydney.

The voyage was long, but on the whole pleasant. The convicts behaved well except on one occasion, when one nearly murdered another by striking him violently on the head with a pumice stone used for scrubbing the decks. For this daring and murderous assault the offender was placed in heavy irons, and next morning the whole of the convicts were paraded on deck, and with my detachment under arms and loaded, on the poop and in the cuddy, the prisoner was brought forward, stripped, and tied to the main rigging, and there received the severe corporal punishment of a hundred lashes. This had the desired effect, and from that day all was order and regularity. We arrived in Sydney on the 2nd March, 1834; the convicts were landed next day and marched to their quarters, and my detachment to the Sydney barracks.

I brought letters of introduction to the governor, General Sir Richard Bourke, from Sir Hussey Vivian, and also from Lord Stanley, then Secretary for the Colonies. With these I called at Government House; but the governor was at that time engaged and could not see me, so I left my letters with the aide-de-camp, who requested me to call next morning. Meanwhile Sydney was in a great state of excitement in consequence of news having just been received of a general mutiny of the prisoners at Norfolk Island, and an attack upon the troops there, with the loss of several lives.

This mutiny had occupied the minds of the prisoners for many months, and was so planned that they were to attack the guards in gangs simultaneously, armed with hatchets, hoes, crowbars, and hammers, on going forth from their prisons to work; they were then to bind their victims and keep them in front, as shields, while others, with the captured arms, attacked the main body of the troops in barracks. They had arranged to treat the free population with barbarity and cruelty too fearful to mention, and to quarter the colonel and the captain alive.

I may mention that it came out in evidence during the trials that more than half the prisoners were for weeks consulting and planning the best modes of attack and of securing their purpose, and settling what to do afterwards, if successful. Their final decision was that an unusually large number should sham illness on the morning fixed for the attack, and so go (as usual each morning) to the hospital, and there secure the doctor and all the attendants, and then wait ready to make a rush behind a corner of the gaol, where a sergeant's guard of twelve men from the garrison attended daily to receive and to take charge for the day of the gaol-gang—amounting generally to thirty or forty of the very worst convicts in double heavy irons. After this they intended to escape from the island by the next Government vessel arriving. There were at this time only a hundred soldiers with a captain and two subalterns of the 4th Regiment on the island, and the prisoners amounted to seventeen hundred of the most desperate culprits on the face of the earth, but happily they were completely defeated, with the loss of only a few lives.

I attended at Government House next morning as directed, and was kindly received by Sir Richard Bourke, and after asking me a few questions about our voyage he said, "You brought me some letters, Major Anderson, and I am told you would like to be actively employed. You have, of course, heard the news from Norfolk Island. I shall be happy to give you the command, if you like." I answered that I myself would much like the appointment, but that I was a married man, and feared my wife would not like going there, after all we had heard of the desperate state of the prisoners, but that if his Excellency would give me an hour to consult my wife I should then return to him with my answer. He said, "Certainly, I will give you till to-morrow morning to make up your mind." I hurried home and told my wife all, and said that I saw no risk in accepting so good an appointment; but she, under the alarm of all she had just read in the papers, said nothing could tempt her to go there. I almost despaired of getting her consent, till at last I proposed that I should submit to the consideration of

Sir Richard Bourke that I would gladly accept the appointment, if he would kindly give me the option of giving it up at once, should my wife dislike to remain there.

He received me kindly, heard my request, and said, "Certainly, I shall not keep you a day longer there than you wish; meantime, I am going to-morrow to my country house at Parramatta, and I shall be glad if you and Mrs. Anderson will spend a few days there with us, and we can talk the matter over." I thanked him for his kindness, and said we should be most happy to accept his invitation; I then returned to my wife much pleased, and next day we went to Government House, Parramatta, and were very kindly received by the governor and his daughter. We remained there three days, and his Excellency took much pains to persuade my wife that there was no danger in going to Norfolk Island, as we should always have a sufficient number of troops to ensure our safety, that the climate was the best in the world, and our accommodation very good, and far beyond anything we could desire or expect. On leaving, the governor desired me to come to him next day in Sydney, saying that I should then receive my final instructions. I did so, and was told to hold myself in readiness to embark in a few days, and that my first duty on arrival should be to take depositions against all the convicts who were implicated in the late mutiny, and to transmit the same to the Colonial Secretary for the decision of the Attorney-General. I was then sent to the court to be sworn in as a magistrate of the territory, and finally told that the Government schooner Isabella would be ready to receive me and my family in a few days, and to sail at once for Norfolk Island.

We embarked on the 12th March, 1834, for my important command. For the first two or three days we had pleasant weather, but then it blew hard, with the wind right against us, and was very boisterous for a week. Our provisions now became short, and from this and the severity of the weather we were very much inconvenienced, but at last had a favourable change and made Norfolk Island in safety, and fortunately on a fine calm day; for in bad weather the landing there is always dangerous. I was received on the beach by a guard of honour of the 4th Regiment and by Captain Foster-Fyans, who was then acting-commandant (Colonel Morrisett and his family having previously sailed to Sydney). Captain Fyans invited us all to his quarters to breakfast, and an excellent one we had; nor must I omit mentioning how our dear children enjoyed the abundance of cream and fruits set before them, after the hard biscuits and salt pork which was their only food on board.

After breakfast, Captain Fyans took us to Government House, with which we were much pleased. It was a substantial building of one story and standing conspicuously by itself, on high ground; the rooms were numerous and well proportioned, the whole premises at the back being secured within a high wall and the windows in front by iron bars. Thus the whole residence might be considered (in case of an attack) a fortress; there were also in front of the house two eighteen-pounder guns mounted, and the military barracks were not a hundred yards distant. I may add the prisoners' gaols and other buildings were within a thousand yards, and the guns before the house commanded the whole. The more we saw the more we were delighted with our future quarters and prospects. By this time a considerable portion of our baggage had been landed and was arriving fast at Government House, and before night we were as well settled and comfortable as if we had been there for months.

Chapter 2

Norfolk Island

Next day I assumed my duties, and proceeded at once to take depositions against the prisoners charged with the late mutiny. As is usually the case on such occasions, many of the convicts concerned turned King's evidence, and the most willing of all these informers was a desperate and cowardly villain named K——, who was at one time a captain in our navy, and after various crimes was at last transported for forgery. He had been many years a convict, and was always foremost in every crime which promised him a chance of escape, yet when detected always turned King's evidence; but still he was trusted by his companions on account of an extraordinary influence he had over them, and on this occasion chiefly because he was the only one of them who understood navigation, and could steer to a place of safety in the event of success in capturing the island and gaining the shipping.

Of course he took the lead, and under his instructions the whole plan was for months secretly and most ably arranged; consequently his evidence, and that of many others whom he named, and who willingly came forward to save themselves, confirmed without doubt the guilt of all the leading conspirators, so that in a few days the depositions taken by me were complete against about fifty of the most daring characters. For six weeks all went peacefully, all the prisoners concerned being kept heavily ironed in gaol, awaiting the result.

In the meantime we continued making ourselves comfortable, daily visiting and exploring various parts of the island, and each day made us more happy in our lot. The island is evidently of volcanic origin, and abounds in valleys in every direction, and in each of these there is a stream of most pure crystal water. Lemons and citrons of the very best kinds grow everywhere, and are so common in every part of the island that many are allowed to drop from the trees and rot. Guavas and Cape gooseberries are equally common, and at one time oranges were in abundance; but my predecessor had all the trees destroyed, as affording too great a luxury to the prisoners! By convict labour excellent roads have been made everywhere.

The climate is the best in the world, with always a bracing air, never too hot nor too cold. There were many hundreds of cattle and some thousands of Government sheep on the island, so that all the free population had a ration of fresh meat daily, and the officers were allowed to buy as much more as they wished, and flour also, at the commissariat, at a nominal price, never exceeding two pence the pound. All the officers had also gardens and convict servants to work them. All had likewise as many pigs and poultry as they chose to rear. My garden at Orange Vale was a splendid one, abounding with everything one could desire. We made about four hundred pounds of the best coffee annually, and many hundreds of pounds of arrowroot. My pigs and poultry were kept near Government House, together with dozens of turkeys, geese, guinea-fowls, and ducks. All our stock was fed from the refuse of the prisoners' breakfasts and from damaged corn, so that we incurred no expense by keeping such numbers. We made the best bacon that was ever known, and in large quantities, but could not succeed in making hams. When the convict servants failed in this, our medical men tried to secure success, but never succeeded; there was something in the air which caused them to decay. We had tradesmen and mechanics of every kind, and were allowed to have our boots and clothing of every description made for us. The woods of the island were very beautiful, and supplied material for handsome furniture of every kind.

All these advantages I had as commandant without any limits, but no officer could get anything done without a written requisition to me. The public dairy was near my house, and every officer, soldier, and free person on the island got a daily allowance of milk and butter. With all these advantages we lived most comfortably and almost for nothing.

The troops behaved remarkably well. We had only six court-martials during the whole period of my command. All the soldiers had gardens near their barracks, in which they grew all sorts of vegetables; they were also allowed to keep fowls. This not only kept them in excellent health, but gave them employment, and they were always at hand and ready for any emergency which might arise.

At last a ship was reported in sight, and proved to be his Majesty's ship *Alligator*, Captain Lambert, with Judge Burton and a military jury on board, for the trial of the mutineers. They were at once landed, the judge and some of the officers taking their quarters with me, the others with the officers of the garrison. Our carpenters were then set to work to prepare a spare room in the prisoners' barracks as a temporary court-house. This being soon completed, the trials commenced next day, and were continued day after day for a fortnight. Fifty of the leading conspirators were found guilty: more than half the number were sentenced to death, the others to transportation in irons for life. During the whole of this time the frigate was moored off the settlement, within easy range, in case of any fresh disturbance. Two days after the trials, Judge Burton spoke to me officially, and said he had the power of ordering some of the worst of the prisoners who were sentenced to death to be executed at once, before the frigate left, but that he would prefer not doing so till the Governor and Council saw the proceedings, provided I felt sure I could be answerable for their safe custody in the absence of the frigate. My answer was that I felt no fear about their safe custody, and had no hesitation in taking the responsibility; he then said, "We had better put all this in writing. I shall at once write to you on the subject, and let me have your answer as soon as possible." He did so, and in an hour had my answer. Judge Burton and the military jury sailed next day.

They had not been gone twenty hours before I received positive information through my police that another general mutiny was brewing, with the intention in the first instance to attack the gaol and release all the condemned prisoners. This was startling, but I decided to wait for further proofs. Next morning I had the names of about fifty of the new conspirators brought to me, and as most of them were well known to be desperate characters, I gave instant orders for their arrest. They were heavily ironed, and confined in different parts of the gaol, and, as I fully expected, two or three of them offered to give me evidence. I had them brought before me and examined, and each satisfied me that efforts were being made for a general rising to rescue the condemned, and that it was checked just in time, before more serious consequences could follow. I now told the informers that they must be sent back amongst the others, so as to deceive them, and make them feel sure that they had made no disclosures as to the guilt of their comrades, and that when all was over they would not be forgotten. Had I not done this, these men would have been marked afterwards by every convict on the island as informers, and would have been sure of vengeance in some way, sooner or later.

After these precautions all was peace for two months; then the Government brig Governor Phillip was reported. Our usual armed boat was sent off, and brought back as passengers the Rev. Mr. Styles, the Rev. Father McEncroe, and the hangman, and dispatches for me ordering the execution of thirteen of the most guilty of the mutineers. All the others were commuted to hard labour for life. It was left to my discretion to carry out these most distressing executions at such time and in such manner as I deemed safe, taking care that all prisoners on the island should be present, and that the condemned should have the presence and benefit of their respective clergymen for at least three days before the execution.

I issued written orders proclaiming my warrant and authority for the execution, naming the unfortunates who were doomed to die, fixing two mornings for carrying out the sentences, and ordering one half of the convicts to be marched from their barracks and formed into close columns in front of the gaol, on the walls of which the gallows was erected, while the other half of the convicts could see from the barracks all that was going on. This was the order for the first day, when seven of the culprits suffered, and the remainder were disposed of in the same way the next morning.

Before the execution I addressed the convicts, and said that if they attempted to move or to show any sign of resistance the officer in the stockade had my positive order to open fire on them at once. These preparations being all completed, the seven men were brought forward, dressed in white and attended by their clergy. They were composed and silent, and in a few seconds all was over. Not a word, not a murmur, escaped from the assembled mass. The following morning the same arrangements were made for the other half of the convicts to witness the execution of the remaining culprits, and all passed over as before. From that time order reigned on the island during the whole of my government, from March, 1834, to April, 1839.

Chapter 3

Sunday Services at Norfolk Island

The Rev. Mr. Styles and Father McEncroe remained a fortnight with us, and took much pleasure in exploring the island. They left, promising to use their best endeavours to have clergymen sent to us, but none came for two years after this. On my arrival the only Sunday service we had for the prison population was more a mockery than a benefit. All the convicts, whether Protestants, Catholics, or Jews, were paraded together and marched up in single file to a field strongly fenced in, and there locked up. Then an officer stepped forward to the fence and there read the prayers and litany of the Church of England, not a word of which could be heard by the prisoners. They were then marched back to their prison yards, and there locked up for the remainder of the day. The troops and free population had prayers read to them in the military barracks. I renewed my application for clergymen, but the answer invariably was that none could be found to take up the appointment.

This distressed me much, and, looking over the register of the convicts some time after this, I discovered that one of the number was transported for forgery while actually a chaplain on board an English man-of-war, and also that another had been educated as a Roman Catholic priest. These two men had behaved well since their arrival, so I thought it possible I might make something of them.

I sent for Taylor and told him that I had discovered the cause and offence for which he had been sent there, and I was glad to hear he was now considered a steady man. I then spoke of the sad position of our convicts from their need of religious teaching, and said that I considered what was now being done a mere mockery, and that it was doing more harm than good; also that I knew what he had been, and what he could do if earnest and willing; that I would remove him from the other prisoners, give him a comfortable hut to live him, plain clothes, and a convict servant to attend him, and finally, if I saw hopes of doing any good, that I intended without delay to build a temporary church for him, and place there a pew for myself and my civil officers, that I might have the opportunity of hearing him occasionally and judging for myself. He was delighted and appeared most anxious and earnest. I dismissed him with the hope that he would seriously ponder over all I had said, and pray to God to assist him and to sanctify his endeavours.

I then sent for the other, and spoke in the same way to the same effect; he also most gladly and willingly entered into my wishes and promised much. That same evening I put them both in my written orders to be separated at once from their respective gangs, to be quartered by themselves, and to read the services of their respective Churches to the prisoners. This gave general satisfaction, and on the following Sunday the Protestants were separated from the Catholics, and each division marched to their respective places of worship, where the services were read to them for the first time. This was continued every succeeding Sunday with such success that pulpits, altars, and pews were soon built and forms provided sufficient for each congregation, and in due time I made it my duty to attend occasionally at either service, and I was always much pleased with the order and regularity which prevailed in both churches. The soldiers and free population continued their worship as usual at the barracks.

These arrangements succeeded so well that I reported the whole to the Government, and by return of mail I had the satisfaction to receive the Governor's approval of all my proceedings and his desire that the same arrangements should be continued, as he could not then prevail on any clergyman to go to the island. In course of a few months I became quite convinced that our humble endeavours were doing much good, that our acting ministers were conducting themselves well, and that they were respected and looked up to by their former associates. I therefore made a report of this to the Government, and recommended that they should be further encouraged by a salary of one shilling a day and the promise of a commutation of their sentence hereafter, if recommended by me for continued good conduct. All this was granted, and I had much pleasure in promulgating the same and in carrying it all out.

For two years this went on with much success, and greatly to my satisfaction. Then we got into trouble. Two convicts attempted the lives of two of their comrades, on different occasions, without any previous cause of quarrel, and, as they afterwards admitted, for no other reason than that they were tired of their own lives and wished to get hanged! The first attack occurred when the convicts were going out from their barracks after breakfast to their daily work. This gang was going to farm labour, armed with field hoes. Without a word of previous warning the would-be assassin raised his hoe and with all his might struck the convict in front of him on the head, knocking him down insensible with a fearful wound in his skull. The unfortunate sufferer was at once taken to the hospital, and remained unconscious for many days. When he recovered he clearly proved that he had never had any previous quarrel, nor had he ever even spoken to the prisoner before. The other case was that of a convict who had got away from his gang and concealed himself in the hut of one of the overseers (who was allowed to live and remain there at night), and whom he had determined to murder. He hid himself behind the door, and when the overseer entered he knocked him down senseless, but happily two other men followed, who at once secured the culprit. These cases were too serious for me to deal with, so I took the necessary depositions and sent them on to the Colonial Secretary for the consideration of the Attorney-General, and by the next arrival of our ship Judge Plunket and a military jury came for the trial of these two men. They were found guilty and sentenced to be hanged; the execution took place a few days later, in the presence of all the convicts, without a murmur. One of the men who had been assaulted recovered in due time, but the other died, and from that day we never had another serious crime.

I discovered from the registers that I had about one hundred former soldiers (amongst the prison population of seventeen hundred) from regiments in India and the Australian colonies, all transported for assaulting or threatening the lives of their officers, generally while under the influence of drink. I ordered them to be all paraded for my inspection, and then said to them, "I find you have been soldiers. I know that you were sent here for assaulting, or threatening to shoot, your officers in your drunken bouts. I have examined your registers and know all about you. Now, I am a soldier, and consider you are still almost soldiers, so I shall at once separate you from your present associates, whose offences have been very different to yours. Most of them are criminals of the worst and deepest dye—murderers, thieves, and assassins. Their companionship must in time degrade you and make you desperate, and perhaps as bad as themselves. I shall therefore try to save you as far as I can. I shall place you in rooms and messes by yourselves, and in separate working gangs. More than this, if I require you I shall put arms in your hands; for you have been soldiers (as I am now), so I shall not be afraid to trust you if I require you!"

They began to cheer with delight, which I at once stopped, reminding them that I could not allow any such expression of their feelings, and that from them I must expect perfect discipline and quiet obedience; then I concluded by saying, "In this way I mean to trust you so long as you behave yourselves and deserve my support, but if I ever again, from this day, see you speak one word to, or associate in any way with, your former companions, back again you go to them, there to remain always as outcasts in misery." They were delighted, and could only with difficulty restrain expressions of their joy, and from that hour my arrangements were carried out admirably to the last. The mass of prisoners were, however, for some time, much annoyed by this arrangement and partiality; but after longer reflection, I was assured, they were glad of it, as it showed them that reason and justice ruled the commandant, and that belief caused a general disposition towards good order and regularity.

I may say that, taking them as a whole, and remembering their previous numerous and great crimes, the convicts during my superintendence behaved wonderfully well. After the capital crimes already mentioned we had but individual offences, such as striking or threatening their constables and overseers, disobedience of orders, and neglecting their work. For these misdeeds they were always sent to gaol, and brought before me in petty session next morning, and if found guilty, on sworn evidence, sentenced to a week or fortnight, a month or two months' imprisonment in irons in gaol, according to their offences. In more serious and aggravated cases they were sentenced to corporal punishment—from fifty or a hundred to three hundred lashes; but these instances were comparatively few, and always avoided if possible. The average of the latter punishments, in my time, was from seventy to seventy-five cases a year, whereas in Colonel Morrisett's time they always exceeded one thousand, though he had not at any time more than twelve hundred prisoners, while with me their number increased year by year, until we had over seventeen hundred.

Chapter 4

Life at Norfolk Island

I never had a complaint, except one, against my soldier convicts. While riding one day some distance from the settlement, the superintendent of agriculture, Mr. MacLean, came galloping after me and reported that there was a mutiny amongst the soldier gangs, or rather that they had refused to do their work. I at once rode back to where they were, and found them all idle and standing still. I ordered them to their work, when one of them named Shean (formerly of my own regiment) stepped forward with his hoe in hand (with which farm-implement they were all provided), and in a loud and angry voice attempted to argue their grievance with me. I instantly rode at him, and, with a heavy stick in my hand, knocked him down and rode over him, saying: "You, who know me long and well, you dare to raise your voice against my authority, you dare to disobey my orders! Get up, and go back at once, every one of you, to your duty!" When he recovered, he begged my pardon, and without another word or murmur they all went back to their work. During this disturbance there were three or four hundred other convicts working in sight, looking on, awaiting the issue, and who doubtless would have joined the soldiers' gangs had anything more serious taken place.

This was the first, the last, and only prisoner I ever had

occasion to lift my hand to while on the island. As I have already said, I always found the soldier gangs very willing and obedient, and most thankful for the promise of being trusted with arms should any general outbreak take place which might justify me in calling for their assistance. I had indeed a soldier's feeling for them. For their continued good conduct I recommended many of them at various times to the Government for pardon and restoration to their regiments, which was invariably granted, and among that number was the above-mentioned Daniel Shean, of the 50th Regiment, who afterwards served with me in India, and I found him a good and faithful soldier. He was finally caught and eaten by a crocodile in the Ganges, while bathing, on our passage from Chinsurah to Cawnpore in 1842.

It was almost my daily practice to examine and study the public records and registers of the prisoners and to select from them the names of all men who had for years been noted for good conduct. When I found life prisoners without any charge against them for six or more years, or prisoners of fourteen years behaving well for three or more years, or prisoners of seven years without a fault for two or more years, I recommended them to Government for commutation of their sentence. These recommendations were always attended to and granted, and when received by me were promulgated in my public written orders and read to the prisoners. This had the best effect, and convinced them all that it was never too late to reform, and that the commandant had a constant and friendly eye over all, even the worst of them. When these commuted sentences were without fault, and nearly completed, I had them pardoned altogether and removed to Sydney.

About this time the officers and soldiers of the garrison applied to me to have a temporary theatre erected for them, as they confidently hoped they could make up a respectable *corps dramatique*. I entered at once into their wishes, and promised them every encouragement, feeling assured I could not do too much to amuse them; and having plenty of wood and labour at hand, a very comfortable theatre was soon built, with dress boxes and pit, and no sooner finished than our first play was announced. I forget the name of the piece, but our principal performers on that occasion and for many months afterwards were my secretary, the Hon. Mr. Pery, Sergeants Cairns and Duff, Privates Thomas Smith and John Swap, with occasionally Lieutenants Wright, Gregg, and Needham, and some others, and as many minor performers as they needed from the troops. Excellent scenery of all kinds was painted by artists amongst the prisoners, and the orchestra was composed of about half a dozen well-conducted convicts, who played the violin and clarions well. The dresses were generally of coloured calicoes and such other imposing materials as they could find. As the acting was always good, this was a continued source of amusement and delight to us all for years.

On one of these nights, in the middle of the performance the "alarm" was sounded. On this occasion many of the performers were acting as women, and of course were dressed accordingly. When an "alarm" is given, no delay is allowed, but all have to assemble as they are. On this night (which by the light of the moon was as clear as day) the "corps dramatique" ran as they were for their arms, and so appeared on the public parade amidst roars of laughter, for their appearance was certainly comic in the extreme, and such a sight of armed warriors in petticoats as never was witnessed before. The "alarm" proved a false one, occasioned by a young soldier firing from his post at the prisoners' barracks on hearing some quarrel amongst the convicts within.

I have already said our roads were excellent all over the island, and the scenery most beautiful and romantic. This encouraged us to pass our time very often in picnics in every direction. There was not a pretty spot at any distance beyond the settlement without a nice bower with tables and seats for our accommodation; and in one or other of these paradises we used to assemble and pass many hours. We had also frequent dinner-parties and dances, and as I had then finished building the new military barracks and hospital, the latter (for we had no sick) made a most excellent and commodious ballroom. The officers of the garrison had a comfortable mess, and were most liberal in their entertainments. In a word, we all agreed well together, and although most of our young men were tired of the limits of our little island, and compared their situation to the monotony and confinement of ship life on a long voyage, I do think we were all very happy, or ought to have been so.

They had also other amusements—fishing, shooting, etc. Phillip Island lay within four miles of us; it is a high land about a mile long, and abounded with wild pigs, wild fowl, and a variety of birds, the most remarkable being the Phillip Island parrots, which were never seen in any other part of Australia. Whenever any of the officers wished for a day's sport there, they had a boat at their command for the day. Starting early, with a good supply of provisions, they were obliged to return before sunset, and generally brought back with them some half-dozen or more pigs, besides other game. In like manner, when they wanted a fishing excursion a boat was provided, and in a few hours they generally returned with dozens of fine fish, caught over known coral rocks. By this time I had an open carriage (made on the island), and as we had many Government horses doing nothing, I wrote to the Colonial Secretary requesting to be allowed to purchase two of them. The answer was that they could not be sold, but that the Governor had no objection to my making use of them as much as I liked. I then sent to Sydney for a double harness, and from that time we had our carriage, and a first-rate (convict) coachman.

In September of this year my dear brother John paid me a visit from India; he was then a colonel of the Madras Army. We had not met for thirty-four years, and our pleasure was now very great in seeing each other. I never saw him again till 1858, and that was our last meeting, for he died soon afterwards at Folkestone.

Reports had now reached Sydney of the better behaviour of our convicts, and we were spoken of with hope and confidence for our continued improvements, so the fear and dread of coming near us, and of residing at Norfolk Island, became daily less. The Rev. Dr. Gregory and Father McEncroe, both of the Roman Catholic Church, offered their services to the Government in Sydney, to go and reside permanently with us, and their services were at once accepted. They came to us by the next trip of the Governor Phillip, and right glad was I to receive them. They soon became very popular with us all, and did much good. Then the Government sent down the Rev. Mr. Sharpe, of the Established Church, who on his arrival took charge of our Protestants.

I may here mention that my power was absolute, and that I could remove any of the civil officers at pleasure from the island, but I am happy to say I had but once occasion to exercise my authority. It was officially reported to me that Mr. MacLeod, the superintendent of agriculture, had been trafficking to a considerable extent with the convicts, actually receiving money for them in letters from their friends in Sydney. At first I could not believe this possible. I then got proofs beyond doubt, consisting of letters addressed to Mr. and Mrs. MacLeod from persons in Sydney with several sums of money enclosed for convicts therein named. After some consideration I sent for MacLeod and told him the charges brought against him; he at once boldly denied them, and said there was not the slightest truth in them. I then showed him the letters from Sydney; this staggered and surprised him, but he said he had never seen them before and knew nothing about them. I had no other course left but to suspend him from his duties and send him back to Sydney by the very first opportunity, but it was not till six weeks later that the Governor Phillip arrived, and in her he and his family left the island—but before that he gave me some more trouble.

CHAPTER 5

Mangalore Cattle Station

Just as these charges were brought against MacLeod, the hired schooner Friendship arrived off the island with Government provisions and stores, and after exchanging signals she made fast to a large buoy and moorings which had been laid down some months before by his Majesty's ship *Alligator*. Captain Harrison and Mr. Bull then landed to report themselves, and I asked them to dinner. When this was over I told them they must return at once to their ship and look to her safety, that I should send a trusty constable and a few men with them, and that, should it come to blow hard, they must immediately slip away from the moorings and stand out to sea until the weather moderated.

They returned to their vessel, but about midnight it blew very hard, and at daylight we had a very strong gale; the schooner was then seen dragging the moorings and drifting fast towards the rocks in front of the settlement, yet not a man could be seen moving on board. I was in bed at this time, and one of my chief constables came and informed me that the schooner was drifting fast on to the rocks, and the surf on the beach was running so high that it was impossible to send out a boat, adding that no man could be seen on board, and that they must all be asleep. I dressed hurriedly, and sent to the military barracks for our gunners and some ammunition for our great guns, and as soon as they arrived we fired round after round over the schooner, yet not a man appeared on deck. At last they heard us, and attempted to make sail. But it was too late; for by this time the ill-fated vessel was amongst the breakers, and in a few minutes more was broadside on the rocks, and soon became a total wreck. The crew and guard got on shore in safety, and our next efforts were to save the cargo, and for this purpose some dozens of prisoners volunteered their services, and went off through the surf, up to their waists, some to their necks, and succeeded in getting on board. Captain Fothergill and about twenty soldiers followed to protect the property and preserve order.

There was a large fire seen burning in the caboose on deck, the sparks flying about everywhere, and repeated cries were heard that there was powder on board. The kegs were soon discovered and thrown overboard; the prisoners then got into the hold, and managed to get small and large cases of stores on deck, then handed them over the ship's side to gangs of prisoners on the rocks. In this manner the whole cargo was safely landed without any loss or damage, but the unfortunate ship became a greater wreck every day. At last what remained of her was towed into the boat harbour, and several attempts were made to patch her up, but all to no purpose, and at last all efforts were abandoned.

I had to quarter Captain Harrison, his crew and passengers on the different civil and military officers and free constables, and I took Mr. and Mrs. Bull to Government House. Captain Harrison became the guest of the military officers, and we all endeavoured to make them as comfortable as we possibly could. About a month afterwards it was reported to me that Captain Harrison talked of selling the wreck and other materials and stores belonging to the vessel, and that MacLeod, the late superintendent, was in his confidence, and was advising him to do so. I took no notice of this at the time, but from other information I clearly saw the object was to defraud the underwriters, as the ship was insured. Captain Harrison had posted handbills over the settlement, naming a day for the sale of the wreck and stores by public auction. I ordered the bills to be torn down, and, sending for Captain Harrison, I reprimanded him for attempting such proceedings without my order, and told him I could not permit any sale of the kind, but that when an opportunity offered for sending him and his crew back to Sydney they should be allowed free passages and room for his stores and cargo also. He appeared dissatisfied, and wished to argue the matter with me, saying that he and others thought it better to sell everything on the island. I begged to know his advisers, but he would not tell me, and from this time he gave me much trouble.

At last the Governor Phillip was reported in sight. I ordered Captain Harrison and his crew and passengers to embark in her for Sydney, and so got rid of them after a detention of seventy days. I also sent MacLeod away beyond my control for ever, and our mail contained my reports to the Government of the wreck, and all details connected with the saving of the cargo, the attempt to sell the wreck and stores by public auction, and my refusal to allow Captain Harrison to do this. I also reported the whole of MacLeod's misconduct, and that I had suspended him from his situation and sent him back to Sydney. I had the satisfaction to receive the Governor's entire approval of all these proceedings. Soon after this several letters appeared in the Sydney papers abusing me, reflecting on my "misgovernment" of Norfolk Island, and complaining of my treatment of the captain, crew, and passengers of the schooner Friendship. I was afterwards assured these letters were written, some by Captain Harrison, others by MacLeod and Mr. Bull, who with his wife left me and Mrs. Anderson with many tears and endless professions of gratitude for our kindness and hospitality during their long stay with us. Of these letters I took not the slightest notice.

Early in 1838 I received a public notification that his Majesty King William IV was graciously pleased to appoint me a Knight of the Royal Hanoverian Guelphic Order for my past services in the field; at the same time I received the Golden Star and Ribbon of the Order. I was indeed proud of this distinction, as it was conferred without any application from me, and I was included in a list of many brave officers specially selected by his Majesty from different regiments for this mark of his royal favour.

Soon after this I received a letter from my brother John, recommending that we should together take up a station for sheep and cattle in the newly discovered district of Port Phillip, saying that he was willing to purchase a few hundred sheep and cattle to make a beginning, if I could find trustworthy persons to go and take up a suitable run and the charge and management of the establishment afterwards, and that he wished to include amongst the number to be employed a Mr. Howell, a young protégé of his. My brother-in-law, Septimus Campbell, had some time before this expressed a wish to retire from the service and try what he could do as a squatter, so I named this chance to him, and offered to recommend him to my brother for the management, and for a share in the concern hereafter if he proved himself capable and deserving of the charge. He willingly accepted, and I wrote accordingly to my brother; I named also three men then in Sydney, who had been until lately prisoners at Norfolk Island. I knew they were not only trustworthy, but also well acquainted with sheep and cattle, as they had been formerly employed as shepherds on sheep and cattle stations. My brother wrote back approval of my proposal and consenting to give Campbell the management of our station, provided he could at once enter on the charge, as he was already in treaty for the purchase of a few hundred sheep. Campbell now sent in his application to retire from the service by the sale of his commission, and I gave him leave to return by the Governor Phillip (then with us) to Sydney, and there he found my brother and Mr. Howell. At that time convict servants were assigned by the Government to officers in numbers according to their rank, and Campbell made an application in my name, and in his own, for three men whom I had named, Joseph Underwood, William Percival, and Richard Glegg. They were at once granted, and most thankful they were for our confidence.

My brother now concluded his bargain for the purchase of a few hundred sheep, a dray and team of working bullocks, and a variety of stores and farm implements, etc.; and having made his arrangements with Campbell, and given him a few hundred pounds for the purchase of cattle, they started for Port Phillip about October, 1838. They went overland, except Campbell, who had decided on going by sea, so as to get down before them. For the first week the overland party got on very well, but after that they had endless difficulties and losses, for Howell gave himself up entirely to drink and was seldom sober, and when his money was expended he actually sold some of the bullocks and sheep. He frequently remained for days and nights at miserable pot-houses quite insensible from intoxication, and when he became sober he was not allowed to leave till he had paid for his folly by giving up as many of his sheep and bullocks as the equally drunken and unprincipled landlord chose to extort from him. Fortunately, our men remained steady, especially Underwood, who now took the lead and the entire charge of our property, and with the other men watched the animals day and night, and never left them; but in spite of all this they lost a number of sheep. Some were stolen, some were knocked up and died, from bad roads and much rain.

At last, after a long journey of two months, Underwood and his two men reached the bank of the Goulburn River, in the Port Phillip district, with about three hundred and fifty of our sheep, the dray, and three or four of our bullocks. They had not seen Howell for some weeks before, and he was drunk at a public-house when they last saw him. Underwood determined on halting and taking possession until the arrival of Campbell. Meantime Howell joined them, but left them again in a few days for a public-house which was on the Sydney line of road, a few miles distant. Campbell directed them to stay where they were, on our future run and station, and to try and extend the boundaries as far as they could, taking care to mark the limits as well as possible, and to report to him by marks or other signs the extent of country they wished to take up, so as to enable him to make a special application to the Government for our right and title to the same. Underwood managed this admirably, and, having had a good knowledge of sheep stations before, he took care to give us a wide range. In front we had seventeen miles on the banks of the Goulburn River, and from twenty to thirty miles in all directions back. By a survey made a few years afterwards, our run was computed at about eighty-five thousand acres. I named the place at once Mangalore, in compliment to my brother, that being the name of his military station in India, of which he was very fond, and so it remains on all charts to this day.

Campbell never stayed at Mangalore, as some pressing business obliged him to go to Van Diemen's Land, and thence to Sydney; so for many months our station and property remained under the nominal care of Howell, but in reality under the faithful management of Joseph Underwood. There was little now to do, for when we took possession there was not one other settler in that neighbourhood, nor nearer than the Devil's River, a distance of more than a hundred miles. There was a miserable public-house and a small store in our neighbourhood known as Seymour, and there all sorts of supplies and provisions could be purchased at exorbitant prices, and they were always ready to trust squatters or their agents, so that Howell had no difficulty in getting what he required. I was still at Norfolk Island during this time, and knew nothing of Howell's doings for many months later. My brother had returned to India, confident with me that all would be well at Mangalore, and telling me, as his last instruction, that I was to consider the whole as a joint speculation, and keep an account of all additional expenditure. I wrote to Campbell and authorized him to draw upon me for any money he required.

We remained happily at Norfolk Island until February, 1839. About the end of the month the Governor Phillip arrived, bringing a detachment of the 80th Regiment under the command of Major Bunbury to relieve the 50th, and with dispatches to me naming the major as my successor as civil superintendent and military commandant of the island.

After our arrival at Sydney I began to hear something about our sheep station and the doings at Mangalore, and that Howell was constantly drunk; so I made up my mind to go to Port Phillip and Mangalore. I left Sydney in a sailing vessel in December, 1839, for Melbourne, and arrived there after a week's journey. Melbourne was then little more than a village, and with only two or three very humble so-called hotels. On my landing I was so fortunate as to meet a

Mr. Michael Scobie, from my own birthplace, whom I had known as a boy; he told me that my worthless superintendent Howell was then, and for some time had been, in Melbourne, and constantly drunk.. Mr. Scobie accompanied me to search for him, and we soon discovered that he lived in a miserable pot-house called the Lamb Inn.

He must have heard of my arrival and seen us approaching, for as we entered he escaped through the back door. After many more hunts we at last got hold of him, and I insisted on his going with us on our journey the next morning. In two days we arrived at Mangalore, where we found our true and trusty men, Underwood, Percival and Glegg, evidently doing their best, but suffering a little from want of tea and sugar and a scarcity of flour. Next day they collected the sheep, and Scobie made a minute muster of all. They were reported all healthy and in good order. He next rode with me round every part of the station, and the more he saw the more he was pleased with the character and capabilities of the run.

What we heard from the men and saw for ourselves convinced us that Howell was not to be trusted in any way with the management of such an undertaking, and that the sooner I got rid of him the better. I now appealed to Scobie, and offered him his own terms if he would remain at Mangalore and take charge. He first said he would willingly oblige me, but that he had a small station of his own near Melbourne, and that therefore he must take time to consider my proposal.

We remained a week longer at Mangalore; Scobie occupied himself during the whole of that time in riding about and gaining additional information. He then consented to remain with me for one year certain, for £100, and one-third of my increase of lambs, provided that I would allow him to return to Melbourne with me for a few days to settle his own affairs. I consented, and we at once signed a written agreement, and Howell was told his services as manager were dispensed with, but that he could remain at the station on a small salary as long as he conducted himself properly and made himself useful, but if not, Scobie had my authority to dismiss him at once. We then returned to Melbourne very much pleased with our arrangements.

Chapter 6

On My Defence

I should have mentioned sooner that when I left Sydney a dispatch was received by the major-general commanding from Major Bunbury, reporting a serious outbreak and mutiny amongst his detachment at Norfolk Island, and that Sir Maurice O'Connell had determined to relieve the 80th at once from Norfolk Island by an equal number again of the 50th Regiment. I was sent for by the governor, and also by the general; and although they gave me no particulars of Major Bunbury's dispatch, I was asked many questions about the soldiers' gardens, when and why they were given to the men, and my opinion respecting them. All this I explained, and said they were established by me with the authority and approval of the late governor, Sir Richard Bourke, as a means not only of amusement and employment for the soldiers on the settlement, but also in order to give them a constant supply of good vegetables.

I was then told by the general that he was determined to relieve Major Bunbury and to send Major Ryan in command. I was not allowed to know more, but I heard it whispered that the outbreak was in consequence of Major Bunbury depriving the soldiers of their gardens and ordering them to be charged a trifle daily for vegetables from the Government gardens, and that, the soldiers having resisted, he actually sent gangs of convicts to root up and destroy the gardens, which at once made the soldiers fly to their arms and drive the convicts away, in open defiance of Major Bunbury's presence and authority. It was also hinted that he blamed me for all this in having granted these gardens to the soldiers, which he considered contrary to, and subversive of, good order and discipline.

Having heard these whispers, I called upon the general and requested I might be informed whether Major Bunbury had attempted to blame me for the open defiance of his authority by his own men. The general again said he could not then enter into any further explanation, but that I should hear all when Major Bunbury returned; I was therefore obliged to be satisfied so far, and I took my leave. Meantime a ship was chartered and ready to take Major Ryan and his detachment to Norfolk Island, and she was to be escorted by H.M.S. *Rattlesnake*, to force a landing if necessary. In a few days I left Sydney, and did not go back for ten days after Major Bunbury had returned, and the first news I heard was that he had not confined nor punished even one man for the mutiny, which displeased the general very much.

Fifteen soldiers were then arrested as the ringleaders and placed in confinement, and in due course were brought to trial charged with mutiny. They were all found guilty and sentenced to transportation for life. I was also informed that Major Bunbury, in his evidence, did not hesitate to blame me for all these irregularities, and for the insubordination and mutiny of his own men! which he stated were the result of "the relaxed order and system and total absence of military discipline" which I had allowed on the island. This was the substance of his evidence, and as I was absent from Sydney during the sitting of the court-martial, my friends took care to tell me of it on my return.

I went at once to Sir Maurice O'Connell and complained, and I requested an immediate court of inquiry into my system and the efficiency or otherwise of my command. The general hesitated, and said he saw no necessity for any such inquiry, as he was perfectly satisfied; but I said I was not, and that as every one had heard Major Bunbury's serious charges against me, it was no more than justice to me, and to my reputation and character as an officer, that an immediate inquiry should take place. He then consented to order a court of inquiry, and next day Lieut.-Colonel French, Major Cotton, and a major whose name I forget, were named for this duty, and directed to "inquire into the system and discipline maintained by Major Anderson during his command at Norfolk Island."

I was allowed to make a statement in detail of my system, daily duties, and discipline. I then called in succession Captains Petit, Fothergill, and Lieutenants Sheaffe and Needham, who served for years with me on the island, and each of these officers stated to the court "that no commanding officer could have been more zealous and attentive to his own duties and to the efficiency of his detachment; that his parades were regular every morning and evening; that the conduct of the detachment was so uniformly good and regular that not more than two or three soldiers were brought to trial while the 50th was at Norfolk Island; that the detachment was inspected once a month, and the barracks and messes were regularly visited by Major Anderson; that if possible he was too strict rather than too easy with his officers and men." Major Bunbury was allowed to cross-examine each of these officers, but could get nothing from them in support of his unfounded charges. The next officer called was Colonel Woodhouse, commanding the 50th Regiment, who informed the court that he "always considered Major Anderson an able and efficient officer, that he received constant reports of the good conduct and discipline of his detachment, and that whenever he had any troublesome officers or soldiers he always sent them to Norfolk Island to be schooled by Major Anderson." The next called was Lieutenant and Adjutant Tudor, who spoke to the same effect. Last of all I called Major Hunter, the major of brigade in Sydney, and he stated that nothing could have been more satisfactory than the official reports from Norfolk Island, and that he had heard from many that the detachment was considered to be in the highest possible state of good order and discipline. I here declined calling any more evidence.

Major Bunbury was then requested to state whether he wished to say anything more, or to call any evidence. He first recalled Captains Petit and Fothergill, and asked them whether they did not think the giving of gardens to the soldiers injurious to military discipline and to their drill and proper appearance as soldiers; they said, "Certainly not." He next asked them whether the soldiers did not sell their gardens to their successors. They answered that they sold their crops, which they themselves had grown and laboured for, but not their gardens. He then called in one or two of his own sergeants, but the only thing he could get out of them was that the soldiers of the 80th Regiment had paid the soldiers of the 50th for the gardens, and therefore considered them their private property. Major Bunbury declined to call in any of his own officers. After some further debate the proceedings were closed. Here we were all ordered to withdraw, and the court was closed for the recording of its final opinion.

I was not then allowed to know what that was, but from the clear and most satisfactory evidence which had been given on my behalf there could only be one opinion on the subject, and it was certainly a most gratifying victory. A few days more confirmed this view of the case. I therefore went to the general and said that I had waited patiently, expecting he would publicly promulgate the opinion of the court of inquiry, but to my surprise he said he saw no necessity for doing so. I told him this did not at all satisfy me, that I felt I had a right to request he would promulgate the opinion of the court, but all my endeavours to this effect failed. I then asked him if I was at liberty to proclaim the substance of my present interview with him. He said, "Most certainly," and on the same day I took care to do so. From that day I had no further intercourse with Major Bunbury.

Many months afterwards, while in India, I received an official notification from the major of brigade in Sydney that the Commander-in-Chief at the Horse Guards had approved of the proceedings of the court of inquiry, and had directed the major-general commanding in Sydney to convey a severe reprimand to Major Bunbury, and to inform him that "if he attempted again to insinuate any such charges against Major Anderson he would be brought before a general court-martial."

Chapter 7

Ordered to Calcutta

Continued to receive good accounts of our station from Scobie, and nothing remarkable occurred during the remainder of that year, until I visited Mangalore to see for myself what he was doing. Having procured six weeks' leave, I left Sydney with Major Serjeantson, and in a few days reached Melbourne. We hired horses, and found our way in two days to Mangalore. I then made a partial inspection of many of our flocks and herds of cattle, and of the improvements that Scobie had made, and was very much pleased with all I saw and heard, and especially with the large increase of lambs and calves. Everything was most satisfactory. I saw at once that I could not have a better manager, and therefore, with the fullest confidence in him, renewed the contract for another year.

On my return to Sydney the first news I heard was that my regiment was about to embark for India. I landed and hurried at once to the barracks, and discovered this to be true, and all preparations already in progress for our embarkation. I found my dear wife and children quite well, but all very sad and excited, and wondering if I should be back in time. This was about the middle of January, 1841, and I arranged with my wife that she and the children should remain in New South Wales until I could leave the service and return to them. We also settled that the two boys should remain at Sydney College, and that my wife, with the other children, should remove and live at Windsor (thirty miles from Sydney). My two boys accompanied me to the ship, and ran back in all haste to be in time at the College for their lessons, and no doubt got uncomfortably heated; but they returned to their lodgings without complaining. About two o'clock next morning we were roused by the landlord, who came to tell us they were both very ill, and that we had better send a doctor immediately. I at once went to our assistant-surgeon, Dr. Ellison, and requested him to go as quickly as possible to see them; he did so, and told us they had scarlatina, which was then very common in Sydney. They became worse, and with the advice of the doctor we brought them home, and now their dear mother gave her whole thought and attention to them; but there was a continued change for the worse, and both became insensible.

The 80th Regiment from Parramatta marched into our Sydney barracks. They asked me and my officers to dine with them, and I went, with a very heavy heart, as I was in great anxiety about my boys. Just as the cloth was removed one of the waiters told me my servant wanted me, and on going to him he said, without any preparation or hesitation, "Master Johnny is dead, sir." I ran home at once, and the sobs of my dear wife confirmed the sad tale. I went with her into the room, and there they both lay, the one dead, the other unconscious, yet I could scarcely believe the fact, for our beloved Johnny was still warm. No medical man was present when he died, nor was his mother or nurse aware that his soul had fled, till they observed he had ceased to breathe. Our agony and sorrow may be imagined but not described.

We retired to bed but not to sleep, and had not been long there before the nurse came and said that she did not believe the child was dead, as he was still warm. I instantly flew to the room, but, alas! her hopes were only a delusion. Next morning we determined on removing the other children, and our good friend W. H. Wright took them at once to his residence at Clarendon House, near Windsor, where my wife was to follow them with our dear boy Acland, should God in His mercy be pleased to spare him.

After this sad and most unexpected bereavement, our quarters became indeed a house of desolation, and the more so from the fact that I was to leave my wife alone and helpless in her sorrow and continued fears for our only son.

Our ships were now ready to sail, but were detained by contrary winds. This delay gave me a little respite, and enabled me to go to Sir Maurice O'Connell to submit to his consideration my helpless situation and my grief, and above all the lonely position of my poor wife, and my hope that he would grant me leave of absence pending my expected promotion, and so allow the regiment to go on to Calcutta, where it would be under the command of Major Ryan, who was to arrive from England at that time. The general heard me with evident sympathy, and expressed his sincere regret for me and for my wife, but would not grant my request. He said that on delivering over my regiment in Calcutta I might then get leave of absence and return, on sending in my application to retire from the service by the sale of my commission. Our boy Acland continued in the same uncertain state between life and death, and was still insensible when I left.

Days and days did I brood over my fears and misery, and I could not conceal my grief. My brother-officers and the ladies on board tried to rouse and amuse me. They were gay without a care, and every evening amused themselves dancing on the quarter-deck. Our voyage was unusually long and tedious. The only cause of excitement which I can remember was that while off Cape Lewin we caught an albatross one fine morning, with a 50th button tied round his neck by a piece of string; this convinced us our other ship, the *Lady MacNaughton*, must be ahead of us, and that our unfortunate captive must have been handled by some of our people before, for in no other way could a 50th button get attached to the neck of an albatross on the wide ocean. Of course we let our prisoner go free again.

On the 17th May we arrived and anchored in the Hooghly. Early next morning we disembarked and marched into Fort William, and were welcomed by Major Ryan and other friends. After this we endeavoured to make ourselves as comfortable as we could in our respective quarters. Mine were with Major Ryan, in a suite of very good and commodious rooms, but the heat was so intolerable that we had neither comfort nor rest. We suffered from the heat fearfully, though wearing only the lightest possible clothing, and from utter exhaustion we expected almost every moment to breathe our last. Next morning we had a visit from the fort major, Major Douglass, who had been for many years in India, and he at once asked us why our punkahs were not going. We said we did not know how to work them. Then, observing our punkah wallas sitting idle in a corner, he "pitched into" them, and abused them for not doing their work; they at once answered they only waited for our orders, and then commenced to pull. In a moment our rooms were full of refreshing and pure air. We then could breathe freely, and from that hour became more reconciled to our lot.

Major Douglass then asked me if I had visited Lord Auckland, the Governor-General, and Sir Jasper Nicoll, the Commander-in-Chief. He recommended me to go at once and report myself and pay my respects to them. He then ordered a palkee and told the bearers to take me to Government House, and then to the residence of Sir Jasper

Nicoll, and back to the Fort. I had to dress in full uniform; the heat was fearful; my thick padded coat was most distressing to me, and I got alarmed, having more than once heard of people being found dead in their palkees from the heat. My bearers, quite unconscious of my fears, jogged on and carried me in safety to the Commander-in-Chief's residence. I was received by Sir Jasper and Lady Nicoll, and after half an hour's conversation about my regiment and voyage I took my leave. At Government House I was most kindly received by Lord Auckland and his sisters, and our conversation was much on the same subject, and I then returned to my quarters.

My first dinner at Government House appeared to me very imposing. The grand apartments were truly splendid. There was a magnificent display of plate—the countless native attendants were most brilliantly arrayed, and all the Oriental splendour round us was dazzling in the extreme. Yet with all this I sat without any dinner for some time, though every one else was being waited on by one or two of their own kitmutgars. Not one of these numerous servants offered to wait on me! At last the young lady who sat at my right asked me if I had no kitmutgar present. I told her I had not, as I was not aware that I could bring my servant to Government House. She then begged me to allow hers to wait on me, and told me that the custom was to take our kitmutgars to attend upon us, at all dinners or other parties.

CHAPTER 8

Life at Calcutta

At Government House the balls were really magnificent, and well worth seeing. The company, of English ladies and gentlemen and of military men in resplendent uniforms, was numerous, but scores of native princes and rajahs, and wealthy baboos in the most splendid dresses and covered with jewels, also constantly attended these brilliant assemblies and gave a wonderfully dazzling effect. The suite of dancing-halls was magnificent, with marble floors, and with dozens of punkahs constantly going to keep all cool and comfortable; and there the young and the gay danced at their ease and without the usual European exertion, from eleven until an early hour in the morning.

The most conspicuous and splendid person at all these parties was Dost Mahomet, the ex-ruler of Afghanistan, who was then a State prisoner at Calcutta. He and his numerous suite were paid the most marked and courtly attentions by the Governor-General, and always invited to every ball or dinner-party, and there, and everywhere else, he was received and treated with all the honours due to a sovereign, and he gained by his courtly manners and easy bearing the respect and goodwill of every Englishman who came near him. He always appeared amongst the crowd in his carriage, every morning and evening in the public course at Fort William, and was invariably saluted by every officer and Englishman, and all these greetings he returned with visible satisfaction. Many if not all the British officers would have gone further and called upon him to show their respect (for he was much liked by every one), but this was forbidden by a Government order, and none but natives were permitted to visit him; these visitors, however, were constant, many princes and rajahs from all parts of India coming daily.

About this time I was invited by the Governor-General to spend a few days with him at his country residence at Barrackpore, and on the first day of my visit the newspapers announced the arrival of a ship from Sydney. This was great news for me, for I made sure of a letter from my dear wife, and having said so to Lord Auckland, I begged to be allowed to take my leave. He most kindly pressed me to remain, and said he would dispatch a man at once for my letters; but I was too impatient, so after thanking them for their kindness I started in all haste for Calcutta, but on my arrival found no letter for me. This was indeed a sad disappointment, and my restless mind at once attributed this silence to the worst and most melancholy cause. After a trying suspense of six months, I received a letter from Major Serjeantson enclosing a long and cheering one from my wife, assuring me of our dear boy Acland's recovery and perfect health, and that she and all the children were quite well and had removed to Windsor, where she had taken a comfortable house. I was again happy and most thankful, and my great desire was to write to my wife to assure her of my joy, and my gratitude to God. But there was then no prospect of any direct ship for Australia, so I was obliged to write via London.

My present letter, sent through Major Serjeantson, was written in April, three months after I had parted with my family, and it will be remembered that when we left Sydney that officer remained there with his own company and our sick then in hospital, and in expectation of receiving and bringing on to Calcutta a number of recruits for the regiment shortly expected from England. With these detachments and some young officers, Major Serjeantson embarked at Sydney on board the ship *Ferguson* at the end of April; but while coming through Torres Straits they were wrecked, and must have all perished, but for the fortunate chance of two other ships being in company with them. These followed the *Ferguson*, which took the lead through a narrow channel, and had just time to bring up and anchor when she struck, and immediately fired guns of distress. This happened before daylight, at four o'clock in the morning.

The boats from the other ships were immediately sent to assist, but the sea began at once to break over the *Ferguson*, and for some time so violently that the boats could not and dared not approach her, and for a time they were obliged to keep at a distance, looking on only. At last, during a lull, they managed to get a rope conveyed from the *Ferguson* to the boats, and by that means another and another. Her long boat was then got into slings and hoisted over the side high up above water. Mrs. Serjeantson and all the women and children were put into it, and after a given signal it was lowered into the sea, the ropes from the other boats having been made fast to it, and then it was hurriedly hauled and dragged through the surf until it reached them in safety. After many cheers they were taken to the other ships and made, so far as possible, comfortable, but after that the sea became so rough that nothing more could be done that day, and in continued fear and suspense both parties remained watching each other until dark.

For the rest of that long sad night the agony and fears of both the rescued and of those more numerous ones still on the wreck may be imagined. It must have been a truly dreadful position. Happily, next morning the sea was more settled, but still too rough and dangerous for boats to go alongside, though by pluck and daring energy they managed to get in succession under the bowsprit of the *Ferguson*, from which man after man of the soldiers and crew were dropped into the boats without any greater accident than a heavy sea breaking occasionally over some of them. This was done from the duty muster rolls, every man in his regular turn and without any confusion, and my dear friend Major Serjeantson, and the captain, Verity, were the last who left the ill-fated *Ferguson*—all reaching the other two ships in safety. But they unfortunately lost nearly the whole of their baggage.

We had now been a few months in India, and some of our officers and many of our men were sick in barracks and in hospital, and a considerable number were suddenly carried off. Major Turner was the first officer who died, and was soon followed by Ensigns Kelly and Heaton. This was during the rainy season; when that passed away the regiment became more healthy.

In October of the same year I was sent for by the Governor-General and told there was every prospect of war with Burma, and that he feared an attack on our position and garrison at Moulmein, in the Tenasserim province, so he had determined to reinforce that station at once. He then asked how soon I could get my regiment ready for embarkation. I answered, "In an hour, without difficulty or inconvenience." He smiled and appeared much pleased, but said he thought that was impossible. I replied that we were always ready, and could embark the same evening if necessary. He then ordered me to go at once to the Marine Board, to put myself in communication with them, and to let them know I was ready to embark my regiment at the shortest notice, whenever the transports were prepared to receive us. I did so, and was told I might make my preparations and expect further orders in the course of that day or the next. A few hours afterwards the orders were issued for the following morning, and punctual to the hour we were at the wharf at daylight, and there found boats to take us to our ships. Mine was a large Government steamer, in which our headquarters and eight companies were embarked, and the remaining two companies were received on board a sailing ship, under command of Major Serjeantson, who had succeeded to a majority on the death of Major Turner. Lord Auckland and his staff attended at the wharf to see us off. My fine regiment was in the most splendid order—not a man was absent, and all as steady as rocks—and reached our ships without the slightest confusion or accident. I was afterwards told that the Governor-General and his staff expressed their admiration of the steady and soldier-like appearance of the regiment, and their wonder and surprise at not seeing one drunken man amongst them; this was so unusual at former embarkations that Lord Auckland actually asked whether Colonel Anderson did not screen his drunken men by keeping them confined in the Fort!

I shall not name the regiment which we relieved on our first arrival at Fort William, but I saw them embarking at the same place, and I well remember my amazement at seeing dozens of the men not only drunk but most riotous and mutinous in conduct and language to their officers. This reminds me of another most creditable contrast between the conduct of the gallant 50th and what I was assured by the best authority had been the conduct of another regiment and other corp previously quartered in Fort William. On our arrival there I found the standing-orders required that every soldier should return to the Fort by sunset, and that none should be permitted, without written passes, to be absent after that time. I considered this a most unnecessary check to the recreations and reasonable enjoyment of good and well-behaved soldiers, and represented this to the consideration of the principal staff officer of the Fort, Colonel Warren; but all my arguments had no effect on that stern and prejudiced officer, who had held his appointment for many years, and strongly maintained that such were the standing-orders of the Fort, and that they could not be changed.

Seeing I had no chance with Colonel Warren, I went direct to Lord Auckland and stated my opinion to him. He heard me with attention, but I soon saw he also was opposed to my wishes, and unwilling to deviate from an old-established standing-order. I told him I thought it was a great restraint upon good soldiers, and that I had heard the men of former regiments in the Fort were in the habit of lowering themselves by ropes and blankets from the walls into the moat, and so escaping; that, in my opinion, such confinement was enough to make bad men worse, and that if his lordship would only make the trial and trust me and my men, by allowing me to give a certain number of written passes for a few hours each night, I would pledge myself to be responsible for their good conduct in town, and for their punctual return to the Fort at the hour required. He hesitated for some time, and, though surprised at my great confidence in my men, he at last gave in, and next day a general order was issued "granting this indulgence on trial, at the special request of Colonel Anderson." That very evening I granted passes till eleven o'clock, and continued to do so daily while we remained at Fort William, without ever having cause to regret it. More than once Lord Auckland expressed his perfect satisfaction and his approbation of the measure; but I never heard if this indulgence was continued to other corps after we left.

Chapter 9

At Moulmein

We now sailed for Moulmein, and found there the 63rd Regiment and four strong and splendid regiments of Madras Native Infantry—all under the command of Brigadier-General Logan, late of the Rifle Brigade, and now of the 63rd Regiment. There was also a considerable force of European and Madras artillery, engineers, and commissariat, and a very imposing naval force under Admiral Cooper.

Our residence at Moulmein was very comfortable and agreeable to us all; the climate was cool and bracing, and under the hospitable rule of our most able and kind brigadier we soon became all intimate and friendly, and the most social dinner-parties at our messes and at the brigadier's became the order of the day. All the Madras regiments had excellent mess establishments, equal in every respect to the Queen's, and their constant and liberal hospitality could not be surpassed by any of our corps. A few days after our arrival in garrison the four Madras regiments invited me and the officers of the 50th Regiment to dinner, and for this purpose they pitched and joined their four mess marquees together into one splendid pavilion, the interior decorated with garlands and evergreens tastefully arranged, and with the spaces filled up with arms and military trophies. The tables were covered with the most brilliant plate and glass, and the lights were numerous and magnificent.

All round the outside was a double row of natives, double torch-bearers, filling up the intervals between the sentries and the bands of the regiments stationed on each side of this stupendous marquee. The effect was truly brilliant and imposing, and no one could approach the gathering without wonder and delight.

We sat down, in all, nearly a hundred officers. The dinner and the wines were excellent, and the attendance of so unusual a number of active native servants in their thin white muslin robes and coloured turbans and kummerbunds was really imposing, and something new to us at a military mess. When dinner was over, and after the usual loyal toasts, the president stood up and proposed a bumper to the health and welcome of Colonel Anderson and the officers of the 50th Regiment. This was drunk with much applause and deafening cheers, the band playing "John Anderson, my joe." I then rose and thanked them with much sincerity from myself and my officers for their hearty welcome and good wishes, and as they all knew my dear brother, Lieut.-General John Anderson, of their own army, I said I felt the more gratified and flattered from the conviction that their good feelings towards me individually were more from their regard for my brother than from any good they could discover in me, and that I was equally free to confess he was indeed much the better man of the two; and here I was interrupted by one of them standing up and shouting aloud, "A d——d deal better fellow than ever you will be!" I instantly turned towards the speaker and told him, and all, that a more gratifying compliment could not be paid me, and that I should not fail to assure my brother of the very flattering and friendly feeling which was thus so publicly expressed towards him. Three cheers then followed for "Old Jock Anderson!" and, not yet satisfied, they now (half a dozen of them) got me out of my chair and on their shoulders, and so carried me round and round the table amidst deafening cheers. The evening continued one of the most social and merriest of my life, and dinner after dinner followed at each of our messes, and many quiet ones also were enjoyed in succession at the married officers' quarters, and always on a large scale at the brigadier's once a fortnight, where that good man and Mrs. Logan made every one happy and at home by their kind and courteous manner and genuine hospitality.

Our military duties were not less exciting and, to me, not less pleasing. We had grand field days and sham fights once a fortnight, with all the troops in garrison present, and I never saw any man handle his force more ably or more effectually than Brigadier Logan. It was quite a treat and a lesson to be manoeuvred by that able and gallant officer. He was a soldier every inch of him, and his ardent zeal for the service was part of his character, but his then most anxious wishes and the object of our expedition to Moulmein were defeated, for although we were ever ready and expecting an attack every morning from the Burmese, they never dared to come near us.

The river Salwen or Martaban (from two to three miles broad) separated the contending forces, for it will be seen by reference to a map that Moulmein is situated on the left bank of the Salwen River, about twenty miles from the sea, and the town and fortress of Martaban, which was then strongly occupied by the enemy, immediately opposite on the right bank of the river, and it was from that place that we expected an attack every morning in boats. We could see their troops distinctly every day parading and marching about in large bodies, with their drums playing and their colours flying, and always with a large fleet of boats moored under their fortifications, as if prepared and meditating a descent. And they could also see our men-of-war and their armed boats pulling about and doing night guard ready to receive them.

In this way we continued for months staring at each other, but in the meantime we made ourselves more comfortable by covering all our tents with matting, which protected us not only from the rains and heavy dews which are common there, but also from the heat and glare of the sun during the day, and we occasionally enjoyed ourselves by exploring and picnic parties in the men-of-war's armed boats up the river; for we were always on the most happy and intimate terms with the officers of our little navy, dining with them now and then and having them as our guests repeatedly. In a word, our sojourn at Moulmein was a very happy and jolly one. We never knew positively the cause of the enemy's hesitation in making an attempt to attack us, but we heard that one or two flags of truce had been sent from our Government at Calcutta up the Irrawaddy with dispatches to Ava for the Burmese Government, and we concluded that terms of amity and peace had been proposed and perhaps agreed to, and this became the more probable when, early in March, 1842, orders were received for the immediate return of the 50th Regiment to Calcutta.

We were indeed sorry to leave Moulmein—the climate was so much cooler and better than India; and we had made so many kind and agreeable friends that to part with them—perhaps for ever—was far from pleasant. A more than usual intimacy took place between our men and the soldiers of the Madras Native Infantry, and they were frequently seen walking and chatting together. Most of these fine-looking men knew and served repeatedly under their own "General Anderson"—and they soon saw by our strong family likeness that I was his brother, and whenever any of them passed me they not only saluted but gave me a warm recognizing smile. When I first saw them I was struck by their fine manly and soldier-like appearance, superior in every way to the Bengal native troops and evidently under better discipline, and now the best proof of this is that when the whole of the Bengal native troops, cavalry, artillery, and infantry, mutinied, and murdered their English officers in cold blood, not one single corps of the Madras native army wavered for a minute. They remained faithful and true to their salt and to their colours, although it was well known, and beyond all doubt, that the leaders of the Bengal mutiny had sent many emissaries and appeals for aid to them.

Chapter 10

Voyage Up the Ganges

I cannot at this moment recollect how we left Moulmein, and here, for the first time since I commenced this narrative, my memory fails me, but I think it was in sailing ships, for I remember that on our arrival off Fort William we were transhipped into country boats next day, and proceeded with the tide up the Hooghly and landed at Chinsurah. There we found Colonel Woodhouse, from Sydney, and a large detachment of recruits and young officers from England under Captain Fothergill, and, what was far more acceptable to me, letters from my dear wife with cheering accounts of herself and my dear children.

I now as a matter of course gave over the command of the regiment to Colonel Woodhouse, and for a time I was, comparatively speaking, an idle man. He, being a full colonel and of so many years' standing, was entitled by the orders of the army in India to the local rank of major-general, and to a separate command. Therefore I felt sure of getting the regiment again before long. We now got into the month of April, and the heat was great and most cruelly trying. We spoke much of the delightful climate of Moulmein, and of the dear friends whom we had left behind us there. The heat and the change of climate soon produced much sickness amongst our officers and men. Fever and cholera prevailed, and we lost many men and Assistant-Surgeon McBean from the latter fearful malady. He was quite well and dined at the mess the night of his death. He sat opposite to me and was in high spirits, and I observed he ate heartily and stayed at table for an hour or two afterwards. On retiring to his room he was suddenly seized with cholera at about two o'clock in the morning, and died in agony soon afterwards. He was buried the same day.

In June we had a fearful storm, or rather a hurricane, lasting two days and nights. Much damage was done, and many ships and river craft driven on shore and totally lost, but it cleared and purified the air, and sickness and cholera disappeared for a time.

Early in July orders were received to hold the regiment in readiness to proceed in country boats to Cawnpore, and about the middle of the month all the arrangements were completed by the commissariat, and a fleet of about 80 or more boats had arrived at Chinsurah for our embarkation. The officers were granted (according to rank) a liberal money allowance to provide their own boat, and they generally got first-rate budgerows, with accommodation for two or three officers, for less than the money allowed by Government, so that the officers of each company might go together or hire a budgerow for each individually, as they liked.

These boats were very comfortable, and had each two good cabins and a bath-room; and the officers' personal furniture of tables and chairs, beds, and chests of drawers left nothing wanting. All the boats were covered with canvas awnings. Each budgerow was attended by two small boats—one fitted with a clay oven and fireplace for cooking, and the other carried the luggage and servants, who kept close to their masters, and came on board without delay or difficulty whenever they were wanted. The men's boats were large, clumsy craft, with matting awnings, and calculated to accommodate from twenty to thirty soldiers, with their arms, accoutrements, and knapsacks. These had each a cooking boat attached, with cooks and assistants. There were also at least a dozen commissariat boats, with live stock and bullocks, sheep and poultry, as well as spirits and wine for the voyage, and there were hospital-boats, where none but the ailing and sick were admitted. The commissariat had also bakers' boats, so that we had fresh bread daily. Before we started each company was furnished with distinguishing flags; mine was distinct, a St. Andrew's Cross on a red ground; and in addition to the commissariat provisions, the officers had their own private stock of poultry, hams, and wines.

With all these means, good accommodation, and creature comforts one might hope for a pleasant change and merry trip on the rivers Hooghly and Ganges, but in course of this voyage we were disappointed. Notwithstanding much variety and fun, we had occasionally to encounter great difficulties. At last we got under way from Chinsurah about the end of July, with strict orders to the boats of each company to keep as much as possible together, and to be guided by their respective distinguishing flags. Any neglect of this arrangement was at once visible and checked. We had our advance and rear guards—the first an officer's budgerow, to point out any difficulties in the river to the advancing fleet, and the rear guard consisting of the captain and subaltern of the day, and one of the men's boats from each company in succession daily. Their duty was to assist any of the boats of the fleet which got into distress from accident or bad management.

When the winds favoured the whole fleet made sail, and when they were against us the boats were towed along the banks of the river, or from the shallow sandbanks by the whole of the crews, by means of ropes tied to the top of the mast. This was very slow and fatiguing work against the strong currents. In this way we some days made fifteen to twenty miles, but generally not more than six.

At eight every morning the halt for breakfast was sounded, and the officers on duty selected the next favourable bank of the river for securing the boats during breakfast. To that spot all the fleet pushed on, and made fast with ropes and pegs. The Hindoo bearers and servants, on account of their religion, would not eat their food in the boats, but landed and made their sacred circle for cooking and eating on shore. Half an hour was allowed for breakfast, and the same time for dinner. At one o'clock the halt for dinner was heard, and the officers again selected a safe place. Frequent interruptions were occasioned by stress of weather, and the loss or absence of one or more boats, and we had many severe and sudden gales, which caused not only the upsetting but the total loss of several boats, and in two instances the drowning of a few unfortunate soldiers and women.

At Dinapore we halted and dined with the officers of the 21st Fusiliers, and a most happy evening we had with them. We also had opportunities of visiting the principal towns on the banks of the Hooghly and Ganges, viz., Barrackpore, Dinapore, Monghyr, Patna, Benares, Ghazipore, Mirzapore, Allahabad, and several other places. At Benares we were most hospitably received and feasted by the rajah at his splendid country residence, after the English fashion. There we had also a severe gale at noon-day, which carried my budgerow away from its mooring down the stream, but I managed to jump out of one of the windows up to my shoulders in the river, and fortunately got safe on shore, but of course with a good ducking. For some hours before this we dreaded a storm; the clouds were dark and heavy all the morning, and so visible was its approach that we got alarmed and landed our tents and all our baggage on the banks of the river for safety. These precautions were not long completed before the gale burst upon us with sudden fury, carrying away my budgerow and many other boats.

About this time cholera again broke out amongst our men, and we lost several, but the greater number of those attacked recovered, owing, no doubt, to our constant change of air. One supposed reason for these attacks was that in most of the confined parts of the river the floating dead and decomposed bodies of Hindoos of all ages were so numerous that they were actually massed together in hundreds where the stream drove them, and where the current was not sufficiently strong to disperse and carry them away. The Hindoos generally disposed of their dead in the holy Ganges, and consequently they were to be seen in all parts of the river and in all stages of decomposition, with vultures everywhere feeding upon them. In halting and securing our boats for the night we always selected good and firm "lagowing" ground and smooth water, and as our large fleet was packed all together, we were sure to find in the mornings dozens of these floating bodies brought up by the current, and jammed between and all round our boats in the most disgusting manner, and we could not get rid of them, nor clear of them until we were again under way and in the open running stream.

During our voyage we saw many crocodiles daily sunning themselves on the various sandbanks which appear in the middle and other parts of the river. They were very wild, but sometimes our sportsmen got a shot at them before they plunged into the water. Some may have been wounded, but we never knew that any had been killed. Our men were strictly forbidden to bathe, for fear of the strong currents, and of our friends the alligators, but, notwithstanding these orders, some ventured on the sly to indulge in this recreation. It was on one of these occasions that

Daniel Shean, a soldier of the light company, who was an excellent swimmer, ventured into the river, and was seen by his comrades soon after to sink, and never to rise again. The firm belief of every one was that he was seized and pulled under by a crocodile and carried bodily away. I omitted to mention that the officers had *tiffin* (lunch) at the men's dinner-hour, one o'clock, and dined after the halt of the day, generally about sunset, and enjoyed themselves afterwards till bedtime either visiting, or resting with every comfort round them, in their budgerows. At last we reached Cawnpore, in the middle of October, having been about three months on our voyage.

CHAPTER 11

In Command at Cawnpore

In spite of our disasters and losses, we enjoyed ourselves fairly well. Our commissariat was perfect. In fine weather, with the wind fair, it was a novel and imposing sight to watch our large fleet under all sail with our gay flags flying. The men's barracks were ready to receive the regiment, and as we had sent on our bearers some days before to select quarters, we all found comfortable houses ready for us on our arrival. The barracks were on a rising open ground near the river. We were allowed lodging money according to rank, which was more than sufficient for the field officers to have each a large and comfortable bungalow, with many rooms, baths, and stables, and the others had similar accommodation by two or three of them joining and living together. There was also a most liberal money allowance for our mess house.

The district was commanded by Major-General Gray, and the station by Major-General Sir Joseph Thackwell, and Captain Tudor of our regiment was A.D.C. to the former. We found the 11th and 31st Regiments of Bengal Native Infantry, and several batteries of European Bengal Artillery and the 5th Bengal Native Cavalry in garrison on our arrival. The 9th Lancers joined us soon after. Nothing very remarkable occurred during the first twelve months of our residence at Cawnpore. We had frequent social gatherings at our respective messes, and our two generals entertained us repeatedly. In January, 1843, Colonel Woodhouse received the local rank of major-general and was appointed to command at Meerut, and I succeeded again to the command of the 50th Regiment.

An unfortunate quarrel took place at Cawnpore between two of our officers, Lieutenant Mowatt and Assistant-Surgeon Bourke, and a general court-martial was unavoidable, the first which was known on an officer of our regiment for thirty-nine years. They were playing billiards after dinner and differed, or rather quarrelled, when some very offensive language was used by both, but more especially by Bourke. A challenge to fight a duel followed from Mowatt, and Bourke declined to fight except with swords. The seconds objected to this, and insisted on pistols as the customary weapon with Englishmen, but Bourke remained obstinate, and would only fight with swords.

Next morning they went out and met at an appointed place, the seconds, or rather Bourke's friend, being provided with both pistols and swords. Here again Bourke insisted on his right to choose his own arms. After a good deal of talk, without any effect on Bourke's decision, Mowatt said, "Well, sir, then here is at you, with swords," taking up one and putting himself in a posture of defence at the same moment. Bourke then declined to fight at all! clearly showing he never intended doing so, and that he named swords in the hope of avoiding altogether a hostile meeting. They then returned to their quarters and communicated all that happened to Captain Wilton, the senior officer present when the quarrel took place, who at once put them both under arrest and reported the whole of this most discreditable affair to me as the commanding officer. Until then I knew nothing whatever of it.

After due consideration I was satisfied that nothing less

than their removal from the regiment or a general court-martial could take place, and I was unwilling for the honour of the regiment to have recourse to the latter expedient. I therefore determined to report the whole affair to Major-General Sir Joseph Thackwell, commanding the garrison, and afterwards, if necessary, to Major-General Gray, commanding the district, and to procure leave of absence for them both for the express purpose of exchanging at once to some other regiments; and in making this request to both these general officers I founded my request on the high character of the regiment and my unwillingness to stain our reputation by a general court-martial, and told them that for thirty-nine years the 50th Regiment had not had one officer brought to trial. Sir Joseph Thackwell heard me most kindly and fully entered into my feelings and wishes, and recommended me at once to see General Gray on the subject; and that officer in like manner agreed to my request, but stated that in making my application to Major-General Sir Harry Smith, the Adjutant-General of the Army, for their leave of absence, I must state the whole of the circumstances, and my unwillingness to tarnish the high reputation of my regiment by recourse to a general court-martial. To this I agreed, and made my application to the adjutant-general accordingly (my old comrade, Sir Harry Smith), which was forwarded and recommended in due course by Generals Thackwell and Gray. But by return of post I received rather a severe letter from Sir Harry Smith, informing me that if the officers named were not fit to serve in the 50th Regiment they were not fit to serve in any other, and ordering me at once to prefer written charges against them, with a view to their being immediately brought before a general court-martial.

I had now no other course left, so I sent in my charges without further delay, and, in a few days more, the general order for the court-martial appeared, to assemble at Cawnpore on a given day. That day soon arrived, and the court-martial assembled accordingly, Colonel Scott, C.B., of the 9th Lancers, being the president. As a matter of duty, I was obliged to appear as prosecutor, and the court being duly sworn and the prisoners arraigned, I was called forward. I commenced my address to the court by lamenting my present most painful and distressing duty, and yet my comparative satisfaction in being able to say that my previous intimacy and friendship with the prisoners, especially with Lieutenant Mowatt, must prove to the court, to them, and to the world that I was in no way influenced by any unkind or vindictive feeling: on the contrary, that I sincerely sympathized with them, and with the distress of every officer of the regiment on this trying occasion.

I then spoke much of the high character and reputation of the regiment, the constant and great unanimity and brotherly friendship of its officers, and the absence for thirty-nine years of any such occurrence; and concluded with an ardent hope that the present would be the first and last occasion of its kind. I then called in succession the officers who were present and witnessed the various matters stated in the charges, and the prisoners having offered nothing in their defence beyond calling on me and several of the other senior officers to speak of their previous character and conduct, the proceedings here closed, and the court was cleared to deliberate on its finding and sentence.

The proceedings were forwarded in the usual manner for the consideration of the Commander-in-Chief, General Lord Gough. I remained very anxious, for the evidence was so clear that I could not but anticipate the result, and I was especially sorry and concerned for my little friend and protégé, Lieutenant Mowatt. At last the General Orders promulgating the finding and sentence of the court arrived. Both were found guilty. Lieutenant Mowatt was sentenced to be severely reprimanded, and Assistant-Surgeon Bourke to be cashiered. These sentences were approved and confirmed by the Commander-in-Chief, but in consideration of the high character and renown of the 50th Regiment, his Excellency the Commander-in-Chief was pleased to remit both sentences and to order these officers to return to their duties. This was most gratifying to us all, for we considered this the highest compliment that could be paid to the regiment, and next we rejoiced to find our friend Mowatt (who was a general favourite) again back in safety and honour amongst us; but Dr. Bourke was not much liked at any time, and now, from his pusillanimous conduct, less than ever. Fortunately for him, his seniority in the service led to his promotion at home to be surgeon of another regiment before anything of this court-martial was known in England, and so he left us for ever soon after.

Chapter 12

The Gwalior War

Shortly after this we had more pleasant and exciting hopes and prospects. War—war! Rumours of war were now heard everywhere, and I soon received orders to hold the regiment in readiness for immediate service. Most of our officers were young, and, with the exception of myself, I believe not one of them had ever seen a shot fired in earnest. All our men were equally strangers to a campaign, but all were full of ardour and zeal, and most anxious to meet an enemy.

As I knew them to be well in hand and in the most perfect state of discipline, I was not less proud of my command and of the prospect of showing (should the opportunity offer) that we were all equal to our duty. In a few days the General Orders detailed the particulars of an expedition against the revolted troops of the Maharajah and government of Gwalior.

Our forces were divided into two distinct bodies. The larger, consisting of many of her Majesty's regiments of infantry and cavalry and European artillery, and a number of regiments of Bengal native infantry and cavalry and artillery, with commissariat and medical departments, was concentrated from the different up-country stations, and ordered to rendezvous at a given place under the immediate command of the Commander-in-Chief, then Sir

Hugh Gough, attended by the Governor-General, Lord Ellenborough, all the headquarters staff, and several general officers in command of divisions and brigades, and all these marched upon Gwalior by a given route. The second column of the army, under Major-General Gray, consisted of the 3rd Buffs, the 50th Regiment, and the 9th Lancers. Also five regiments of Bengal native infantry, two regiments of Bengal native cavalry, and several batteries of European artillery, commissariat, and medical departments marched from Cawnpore and Allahabad and other stations in November, and were concentrated for the first time in brigades on a very extensive plain about half-way between Gwalior and Cawnpore. There we halted, encamped, and remained for nearly three weeks.

Our brigade was composed of the 50th Regiment and the 50th and 58th Regiments of Native Infantry, and under the command of Brigadier Black, of the Bengal army. That officer had for many years held a civil appointment, and candidly confessed that he knew nothing of the duties of a military command and much less of maoeuvring a body of men. At this time General Gray had us out daily at brigade field-days, allowing each brigadier to select his own manoeuvres. I was the second in command of our brigade, and our zealous brigadier used to come daily to my tent, and, with all simplicity and candour, confess that he really could not attempt to manoeuvre his men unless I assisted him by giving him a regular lesson of what he was to do each day. I, of course, consented to do so, and wrote him out five or six simple manoeuvres for each day, and explained them over and over again until he appeared to understand them perfectly.

He used then to leave me and to study his lesson for the rest of the evening, and so well that, when he appeared on parade next day, from memory he put his brigade through the required movements with perfect confidence and without once making a mistake, and he continued this daily, while we remained in that encampment.

During the whole of this time we knew that the main body of our army under Sir Hugh Gough was halted and encamped within twenty miles of us, on a different road to our right, and employed daily like ourselves in fielddays. Native troopers, with dispatches, passed between both divisions almost daily. I never knew the reason of this delay; but it was by many believed to be caused by awaiting the result of pending negotiations. At last we again got en route, our division still keeping the main road from Cawnpore to Gwalior through the Antre Pass, with orders to examine that formidable position before we attempted to enter it. While halted and encamped on the evening of the 25th December our brigadier had a serious accident. He was examining his pistols, when one of them suddenly went off and wounded him severely in the head. This obliged him to be sent at once to the rear to the nearest military station, and I was on the same day appointed by General Gray to the command of the brigade, with the rank of brigadier. Such is the fate and chance of war, and I was delighted with my promotion and prospects, for we were now more than ever certain of meeting our enemy, the Mahrattas, in battle.

But before I go further I must mention that on leaving Cawnpore I wrote to my agent, John Allan, at Calcutta, requesting him to insure my life in favour of my dear wife for £6,000, and while delayed in camp Mr. Allan sent me the necessary papers for me and our surgeon to fill up and sign, to enable him to complete the insurance. This was duly done and the papers returned to him, and by return of post I had another letter from Mr. Allan, saying all was right, that I might make myself perfectly easy. But on the very evening of my promotion as brigadier I received another letter from Mr. Allan, informing me that the insurance office (being now confident of our going into action) had declined the insurance on my life without an additional high premium, and begging to know what he was to do. I instantly wrote to him declining, and saying that I would take my chance, as I had often done before.

On the morning of the fourth day after this, namely, on the 29th of December, we came in sight of the Antre Pass, and General Gray, with a strong escort of cavalry, having been sent on to reconnoitre, soon returned at full speed to inform the Commander-in-Chief that the pass was strongly occupied by the enemy, with many guns in battery. A halt was then ordered, and after half an hour's consultation with his staff, General Gray ordered us to stand again to our arms, and put the column in motion at a right angle to our left, thus intending to turn the enemy's position, and so march upon Gwalior. Some of us felt this a disappointment, but we soon heard that the general's orders were not to attack the enemy unless he attacked us.

We commenced our flank march. There was a ridge of hills running for miles directly parallel to our route, and not many hundred yards from us. We, quite unconscious of any danger, never thought of reconnoitring that ground, which our general decidedly should have done, and continued our flank march with only the usual precautions of our advance and rear guards, and from one end to the other (with our column and baggage, commissariat, and bazaar) we must have occupied a line of road of at least ten miles. Still nothing happened, nothing was expected, until about three o'clock in the evening, when the column was halted for the day and began to prepare to receive our tents and camp equipage. Then we were suddenly roused by bang, bang of artillery in our rear, and soon after by cavalry videttes from the rear guard (still many miles from us) galloping into our lines in great confusion, and frantically shouting that our rear guard was attacked and being cut to pieces.

It was now ascertained that from the time we changed our line of march to the left, so as to turn the Antre Pass, the enemy left that position also, and moved all day parallel to our position and column, keeping the ridge of hills between us until they came over and attacked our rear guard. The "Assembly" was immediately sounded, and we stood to our arms, and reinforcements of native infantry and cavalry were instantly dispatched to assist the rear guard, and at the same time the 3rd Regiment of Buffs, under Lieut.-Colonel Cluney, was sent to the left front over a spur of the ridge of hills already mentioned, my brigade and Brigadier Wheeler's remaining stationary with the general and staff, all ready for orders. Meantime the attack and defence of the rear guard became louder and nearer, and we could hear not only constant discharges of artillery, but regular volleys of musketry and independent file firing, and with these we could distinctly hear a heavy cannonade at a considerable distance. This we supposed at the time to be from Gwalior; but it afterwards proved to be our troops under the command of our Commander-in-Chief, Sir Hugh Gough, engaged in battle with the enemy at Maharajpore.

In a very short time a staff officer came galloping back from Colonel Cluney and reported that the enemy was in great force in his front; on which General Gray ordered me to advance with my brigade to the support, with all speed. We moved off in open columns of companies at the double, and soon found ourselves under the range of the enemy's guns, fired from the other side of the ridge of hills, and the shot now passing over us. When we got close under the rising ground I halted my brigade in close columns of regiments, and the general rode up and inquired angrily why I had halted. I said to load, as I thought it was now high time to do so, for the enemy's shots were still passing rapidly over us. As soon as we had loaded, I advanced the whole brigade as we then stood, in close column of companies by regiments, and as soon as we reached the summit of the hill we came at once in sight of a large portion of the Mahratta army in order of battle, and were instantly under a heavy fire from their artillery and infantry. I rode in front of my column, and deployed them on the grenadiers of the 50th Regiment, the 50th Native Infantry taking our right and the 58th Native Infantry our left. All this was done in double quick and without the slightest confusion, and all as steady as rocks. I then took my station in rear of the centre, and ordered my bugler to sound "Commence firing." Up to that time, so admirably steady were the men that not a shot was fired until the order was given. But then they opened in earnest, and kept it up with the most steady regularity. Meantime, two batteries of our artillery were brought to our right, followed by our first infantry brigade, and these got at once into action, and about half a mile to our left we saw Colonel Cluney and his regiment and a battery of our artillery warmly engaged, and sending shots occasionally into the enemy's columns and batteries in our front.

By this time a number of our men fell killed and wounded, and it was now getting late and the sun about setting. A deep rough and rocky valley separated us from the enemy. My men were falling fast, and I saw no chance of driving our foes before us without crossing the valley and giving them the bayonet. I looked round everywhere for General Gray and his staff, but could nowhere see them. I asked my brigade-major if he knew where the general was, but he did not; so rather than lose a chance, and my men, without doing any good, I instantly made up my mind to advance and at them. I ordered my bugler to sound the "Advance." It was at once passed along the line, and off we went at a rapid, steady pace down the valley, keeping up a brisk independent firing all the while, and receiving the enemy's shot and shell and musketry in rapid succession.

The ground was so rough, with loose rocks and stones, that I and all the mounted officers were obliged to dismount; but with the loss of some men killed and wounded we managed to reach a clear space at the bottom of the valley. It was then all but dark, when, after hurriedly reforming our ranks, I gave the order to charge the enemy's guns, and at this instant I positively saw one of the Mahratta artillerymen put his match to his gun (not many hundred yards from us), the contents of which (grape-shot) knocked me and Captain Cobbam and about a dozen men of my brave 50th over. Captain Hough and two or three men came instantly to assist me, and offered to take me to the rear, where the medical officers were sure to be found; but I said, "No; never mind me: take those guns!" and with many hearty cheers they were all taken in a few minutes, the brave Mahrattas standing by their guns to the last, and refusing to quit them or to run, when positively ordered and pushed aside by our men's bayonets. Move they would not, until they were slaughtered on the spot.

When I was hit I was knocked clean over, and thought it was from a round shot, and that I was, of course, done for. My only care and regret was that my dear wife would lose the intended insurance on my life, and so be left, with our children, worse off than I intended. These thoughts occupied my mind until I was soon after assisted off the field by Sergeant Quick and two soldiers to where the medical officers were attending to the wounded. I had not got far when, by the light of the new moon, just rising, I saw an officer sitting under a tree, bleeding profusely, and resting his head on one arm, and with two or three soldiers supporting him. I inquired who it was, and was told Captain Cobbam, wounded severely in five different places, but still alive. I told them who I was, and that I was then on my way to the doctors, and begged the men to take him there also. A few yards farther on I met the surgeon of the 9th Lancers. He then examined my wound, putting one of his fingers in where the ball entered, and another where it passed out of my body, and then said, "Never fear; you are all right." This was indeed cheering, and enough to make me forget my fears about the loss to my dear wife of the insurance on my life.

He then ordered my escort to take me a little way farther over the hill, where they would find all the medical officers and wounded. We reached them in safety, but faint from much loss of blood. I was again examined, dressed, and well bandaged, and again reassured and told not to be alarmed, as my wound, though severe, was not dangerous. They then put me in a doolie with four bearers and my escort, and ordered them to carry me direct to our camp.

Chapter 13
Wounded and Made Much Of

I now felt much refreshed, and was more pleased with my wound and my good luck than if I had altogether escaped, and, finally, I began to calculate on the honour and glory which must follow our victory, for I was told before I left the field of battle that my brigade had carried all before it. The new moon soon failed, and my escort and I were suddenly left in utter darkness, in a rough and undulating country, without a path or any other means to guide us. It was a bitter cold night, and I soon became alarmed lest we should lose our way and perhaps get into the enemy's lines, and I was not less afraid that my doolie-bearers might bolt and leave me to my sufferings for the night. In this critical situation I called to Sergeant Quick to halt for a moment, and then told him and his men to keep a sharp look out on the bearers, and if they attempted to run, to fire upon them, and, if possible, to try and explain this to them. I then told him that if he heard or saw any suspicious-looking men to let me know at once, but not to attempt to fire until I ordered. I still retained my sword in my hand, and had perfect possession of my faculties, and, if attacked, my mind was fully made up to fight for my life.

We wandered and wandered for nearly an hour without any signs of our camp, or meeting any one, or knowing where we were going. I felt the piercing cold more and more, for there was sharp frost, and I was sensible of losing blood fast through my bandages, for my doolie was well saturated with it. I confess I felt uneasy and alarmed, and in this state I now ordered Sergeant Quick to put me down so as to rest the bearers, and himself to go a little in front and to lie down and listen for any sounds which might reach him. He soon returned and said he could hear nothing, and proposed that we should go on to the top of a rising ground not far from us. We did so, and again I was put down, and the sergeant went out in front again to listen, returning soon with the joyful news that he heard the noise of wheels, as if of artillery or wagons.

I then directed them to take me up and to make for that direction. My teeth were now chattering with the cold, and I felt weaker and weaker, but we managed to get over another half-mile or more of ground, and then I was put down once more, and the sergeant, as before, went to listen. He now returned in all haste, saying he could see numerous lights and was sure it was our own camp! This truly revived and cheered us all, and off we started almost at a trot, and, sure enough, in half an hour more we entered our camp, and soon after I was in my own tent and my own bed.

I was indeed thankful, but so cold and shivering that I asked a native hospital assistant, who soon found me, if a glass of hot brandy and water would do me any harm. He said not the least, so I immediately sent my kitmutgar to our mess-man to get one for me; it was brought, and I did enjoy it, and was just finishing the last drop, when in came our surgeon, Dr. Davidson, and on being told what I had done he instantly pitched into his hospital assistant, and in real anger threatened to destroy him, for giving me the means of causing inflammation and fever! When he got a little cool he removed my bandages, dressed my wounds, and again wrapped me up securely for the night, and put me to bed, leaving strict orders with my bearer and kitmutgar to remain with me, to give me nothing but barley-water if I wanted a drink, and to call him if necessary. I soon became warm and composed, and upon the whole had a good and quiet night, and slept at intervals soundly. Next morning Dr. Davidson examined and dressed my wound, and told me I had had a narrow escape, and that I was now doing well. He also informed me that poor Cobbam was dead; he had received no less than five grape-shot, three in his body and two in his arm, and died in a doolie soon after I saw him.

My wound was about three inches above the left groin, close to the hip, and happily without touching the bone; had it been one inch more to the right it would have been fatal, and instant death, but it pleased God to order otherwise, and I was then, and continue to this day, truly thankful. I said before, I was knocked clean over, and thought it was by a round shot. It struck me on the waist-belt, carrying parts of my belt, trousers, drawers, shirt, and flannel in with it, and the getting rid of these fragments day after day in threads and small particles afterwards caused me more pain than any sufferings from my wound.

These grape-shots were made up in a canvas bag as large as the body of a bottle, with wooden bottoms, and tied at the top with strong cord. They contained from eighty to a hundred jagged balls, nearly twice the size of an ordinary musket-ball, and they were secured by cords wound crossways and about an inch apart on the bag. When discharged or fired the bag is burst at once, and the balls carry death and destruction, broadcast, wherever they fall. My belt being shot through, it dropped off, and with it I lost my scabbard, which I regretted then, and do to this day.

So ended in victory the battle of Punniar, on the night of the 29th of December, 1843. All the enemy's guns were taken, and the survivors of their army fled in utter confusion and disorder, leaving all their baggage and stores and many arms behind. Strange to say, on the same day the main body of the Mahratta army was similarly defeated by Sir Hugh Gough and our headquarters forces at Maharajpore. This was the distant cannonade and firing which we heard before going into action.

For a day or two the doctor would not allow any one to see me, but soon after I had many visits from my brother-officers, and all to congratulate me on my escape, and, above all, on what they were pleased to call my "daring, dashing charge across the valley." Every one spoke of this, and said it had decidedly crowned the success of the day.

At last General Gray's dispatch appeared in the public papers, and after detailing at length the operations of the day, he concluded by saying that "the 2nd Infantry Brigade, under Brigadier Anderson, of H.M. 50th Regiment, by an able and judicious movement turned the enemy's position, charged and took his guns, and so contributed to the final success of the day." My officers were not even satisfied with this, and maintained that much more should have been said, and all blamed Captain Tudor, the A.D.C., who was known to have great influence with the general and to have had much to say and to do in writing the official report of the battle. In short, Tudor was everything with the general, even to the management of his household, and for this he was familiarly and privately called "the chief butler," and during an angry discussion of this dispatch, our paymaster, Captain Dodd (who was a witty fellow), summed up by saying, "Yes, yes; the chief butler forgot Joseph!" It was also urged and maintained that, supposing I had failed in my dash into the valley and lost my brigade or been defeated, General Gray would then have blamed me for attempting to move without his orders, and perhaps brought me to a general court-martial. But all is well that ends well, and so I am satisfied, although I do confess I was, like my friends, a little disappointed at the time.

We remained some days in our encampment at Punniar, and then marched for Gwalior, where we found the rest of our field forces encamped under the Commander-in-Chief, Sir Hugh Gough. The Governor-General, Lord Ellenborough, and his numerous staff were also encamped with our army. Here we continued for nearly three weeks, during which time the most happy and social intercourse took place between the different regiments and corps. We all had our splendid mess marquees and full establishments, wines and luxuries of every kind, and nothing wanting, and public dinners every day followed as a matter of course. The Governor-General and Sir Hugh Gough had also their magnificent establishments, and had their tables crowded every day with guests from each of the regiments. I and many others were confined to our tents and to our beds from our wounds, and could not share in these festivities, but whatever was ordered and good for us we received regularly from our respective messes.

I had another advantage: my tent was pitched so near our mess marquee that I could almost distinctly hear every word that was spoken, and frequently my own name and health drunk with much cheering and applause. This acknowledgment may sound to others like vanity, but I still confess I was well pleased and proud of the good opinion of my brother-warriors.

CHAPTER 14

Return to Cawnpore

The weather still continued bitterly cold, and about daylight on one of these mornings a tall figure, more than usually wrapped, entered my tent, stood in the door, and asked kindly, "How are you getting on, colonel?" I must have been in pain or bad humour, for I bluntly said, "Who are you—what do you want?" He quietly answered, "Lord Ellenborough," so I at once asked a thousand pardons and begged he would walk in and sit down. He continued his inquiries most kindly, and took a chair and sat down by my bedside.

He remained some time with me, and paid me many more visits afterwards. He was also in the habit of visiting all the other wounded officers and men daily, and to the latter (in bad cases) he used to give gold mohurs to comfort them for their sufferings, and these our men prized very much and made into rings in remembrance of our good and popular Governor-General, Lord Ellenborough.

After these battles the Mahratta army submitted to our Government, and in about a fortnight afterwards six or eight thousand of them actually volunteered to enter our service, and were at once formed into ten regiments under British officers selected from the Bengal native forces, and styled from that day "The Gwalior Contingent." They remained faithful to our service until the general mutiny of the native Bengal army, and then I believe they joined the revolt to a man.

About this time I had the happiness of receiving more than one letter from my dear wife, and I made many efforts on my back and in my bed to write to her. My first letter was written a few days after I was wounded, and I managed to get my sash across my back under my arms, and tied to that a piece of rope, secured and tightened to the top of the pole of my tent, so as to raise and support my head and upper part of my body, and so enable me to write pretty comfortably. I was in high spirits, and I gave her a cheering account of my sufferings and a glowing report of my success.

Our encampment was outside the town and fort of Gwalior, and our officers made frequent visits to both, and especially to the fort, which was very extensive and well worth seeing. It is built upon a long and very high range of rocks, and only accessible by one entrance over a drawbridge, the road to which is a long and narrow one, over a minor spur of the same chain of rocks. I was curious to see this formidable fortification, and on one fine morning I was raised from my bed and put into a doolie, well propped up with pillows by my good and trusty friend Captain Dodd. He and a few more of the officers accompanied me on my excursion. The change and fresh air did me great good, and I was much pleased with all I saw, and with the marked and courteous civilities we received from the Mahratta officers and soldiers who garrisoned the fort, for at this time all enmity between us had passed away, and our officers and men were in the habit of meeting them daily and constantly.

I do not remember anything more of any particular note taking place while our army remained before Gwalior. About the last week in January, General Orders were issued for the whole of our forces to return to their former respective quarters, and my regiment commenced its march soon after for Cawnpore. After I was wounded I gave up the immediate command of my regiment to Major Petit, leaving all the daily details to him; but he consulted me in all important matters, and always fixed the hours of marching in the mornings at the time most convenient to me. I was carried in my doolie at the head of my regiment every day, and on halting found my tent all ready pitched in proper position, with my bed and all my comforts prepared for me; for in returning to Cawnpore through a free country our baggage, commissariat, and stores always took the advance of our column of march, and arrived on our camping-ground each morning some time before us.

Such was the efficiency of our native servants that everything, even to our breakfasts, was ready on our arrival. Our march seldom exceeded from ten to fifteen miles daily, so that we were comfortably camped and settled before the heat became oppressive, and the remainder of each day was spent by the officers and men as they best could. I continued to get on as well as could be expected, but as I could only lie in one position (on my right side), my arm, shoulder, and hip became sore and chafed, and this and the jolting of my doolie, and latterly of my palanquin, left me much fatigued each day before our march was over. In this way our daily journey was continued for three weeks, a distance of two hundred and twenty miles to Cawnpore, and there we arrived at last in safety, about the middle of February. I marched in, or rather was carried in, at the head of my regiment, in my palanquin, with our band playing "See the Conquering Hero comes."

All the women and children and the few troops and invalids who remained in garrison turned out to receive and welcome us, and the cheering and shouting which followed, and the welcomes, and "God save the Colonel!" from one and all, were, I confess, most gratifying to me.

We were soon comfortably settled in our old quarters. I was obliged to keep my bed for some months afterwards, but continued otherwise in good health and spirits, and my medical friends assured me I was progressing as well as they could wish. My greatest sufferings were from the constant and unchanged position on my right side to which I was obliged to keep, and from the still continued extraction of threads and small particles of clothing which had been carried into my wound. But at last this painful annoyance ceased, and from that time healing followed rapidly.

In March we received official acknowledgment of our services from the Home authorities, with notices of various honours and promotions conferred in consequence. I had the proud satisfaction of seeing my name amongst the few who were appointed by her Majesty to be Companions of the Bath. My friends Majors Ryan and Petit were made brevet lieut.-colonels, and Major-General Gray a K.C.B., and his A.D.C., Captain Tudor (the chief butler), a brevet major. All other officers of both divisions of our army who had similar claims were either decorated or promoted. I had also the satisfaction of receiving a letter from our agents, Messrs. Cog & Co., informing me that the Secretary of War had been pleased to grant me eighteen months' additional pay for my wounds (commonly called "blood money"), and authorizing me to draw for the same. We were further informed that her Majesty the Queen was graciously pleased to order that the regiments engaged at Maharajpore should bear the name on their colours and appointments, and the regiments engaged at Punniar, that name in like manner on their colours and appointments.

All this good news was very cheering and gratifying to us, and all expressed their readiness to fight and to conquer again. Then followed an order from the Governor-General of India granting to each officer and soldier who served in either of these battles a decoration, a bronze star to be worn on the left breast, suspended from the ribbon of India, and to be made from the cannon captured in these actions, with the words "Maharajpore, 29th December, 1843," on a silver medallion on the centre of the star, for the troops who served there; the word "Punniar," with the same date, for those who fought and conquered at that place; and soon after this I had the honour of receiving mine (one of the first cast), with a kind and flattering letter from Lord Ellenborough.

CHAPTER 15

On Leave for Two Years

About three months after our return to Cawnpore I was able to move about a little on crutches, but not to go to parades for some months more, nor to sleep nor rest on my left side. At last I managed to resume the command of the regiment and to carry on the orderly room duties, and finally to attend parades mounted; but I could not carry my sword, although my wound was by this time quite healed up, for the parts were so tender and sensitive that I could not bear the weight and friction of my sword against my side. My orderly, therefore, always carried it for me.

On the very first ride I attempted to take into the country, my horse shied while passing a bullock-dray on a small, low bridge (not more than three or four feet high), slipping his hind legs over the bridge and falling backwards right over with me. We both came down together, and my right foot stuck in the stirrup, until the weight of my body carried it clear away. My ankle was much sprained in consequence, but I got up at once and managed, with the assistance of two officers who were with me, to mount again and to ride home. I sent at once for our surgeon, who ordered me to keep quiet and to bathe my ankle constantly in cold water under a pump. For days and weeks I thought very little of my accident, but my ankle and leg swelled very much and got worse and worse, with much pain, for many months afterwards.

Various lotions were applied, but I got no better, and as my general health now began to fail, I was frequently confined to bed for weeks, and almost to the house for twelve months.

I now seriously began to think of getting leave of absence, and in December of this year (1844) I consulted our surgeon, Dr. Davidson, accordingly, and he said there would be no difficulty in granting my request. So he at once wrote an official letter recommending me for leave of absence to proceed to Calcutta for the purpose of appearing before a medical board, and that letter I myself (as commanding officer) forwarded to the Adjutant-General of H.M. Forces in India for the consideration of the Commander-in-Chief, and in the next General Orders my name appeared for leave to Calcutta for the purpose above stated.

In January, 1845, I took public leave of the officers of my regiment in the mess-room, and with Captain Waddy (who also got leave of absence), Mrs. Waddy, and their children, left Cawnpore for Calcutta. We travelled together as far as Benares. There I took passage in one of the well-found and comfortable public river steamers, but Captain Waddy and family hired a budgerow and soon followed with the current, but did not reach Calcutta till a fortnight after us. I had previously written to my friend and agent, John Allan (one of the wealthy merchants of the "City of Palaces"), telling him that he might expect me, and requesting him to make every inquiry for passages for us to Sydney or to any part of Australia. He received me most kindly, and insisted on my taking up my quarters under his hospitable roof. He told me there was no chance of a direct passage to Australia, but that he had written to Mauritius and to Singapore to inquire if we could get passages in a vessel from either of these places for our destination.

Meantime I reported my arrival to the military authorities, and was told a medical board would assemble on a given day, and that I had better call on Dr. Murray, Inspector of Hospitals and chief of the Medical Department. I did so, and after a conversation, in which I expressed my wish to be sent to Sydney, where my family then was, he said he was afraid he could not recommend me to be sent there, as his instructions were to send officers who received long sick-leave direct to England. I explained that that would not suit me at all, as to see my wife and family was of more importance to me than even my health. He then said he would consider it and would give me an answer the next day. I called the following morning, and he told me that in the event of my medical board recommending me for leave of absence, he would request I might be sent to Sydney. A few days afterwards I appeared before the board, and after they had asked me a few questions my leave was granted for two years, to proceed to New South Wales for the recovery of my health.

By this tune Mr. Allan had received answers to his letters to Singapore and to Mauritius informing him there was not the slightest chance of finding passages from either of those places to Australia; he therefore advised me to go at once to the Cape of Good Hope, where we would be sure to find vessels for Sydney, as many of the English traders for that port called at the Cape for supplies. A fine ship was ready to sail in a few days for England, touching at Mauritius and at the Cape, so the Waddy and I secured our passages at once, with the understanding that we might leave either at Port Louis or at Table Bay, but when we arrived at the former there was no prospect of a passage for any port of Australia, so we proceeded in a few days to Cape Town. There we landed and took up our quarters at a most excellent lodging-house; with us were two officers of the Madras army, one of whom was a medical man, well acquainted with my late brother, and he was most kind and useful to me. We were there for a week or ten days, and there being still no hope of a passage, we all made up our minds to leave our lodgings and to go together and occupy a very nice and partly furnished house in the country, five miles from Cape Town.

There we lived comfortably for another ten days, when Captain Waddy returned in a great hurry from the town one day to tell us that the ship Penyard Park had just arrived, bound for Sydney; she had put in for supplies, but was so full that he was afraid we should have some difficulty in getting passages. We at once determined to take our chances, no matter how limited the accommodation. Captain Waddy started, intending to go on board and to secure, at any price, the best cabins he could get for us. In a few hours he was back, and told us he had had much difficulty in securing for us two cabins at exorbitant prices—one cabin for himself and family on the lower deck, with scarcely any light or air, and for me, the second mate's cabin, of only five feet long and four feet wide, leading from the quarter-deck into the poop, and where it was impossible for me in any way to stretch myself or lie down at full length. For this I was asked to pay seventy pounds, while Captain Waddy was to pay eighty for his. But we could not help it, and Captain and Mrs. Waddy made up their minds to go at any price, and to put up with any inconvenience, rather than lose the chance and remain behind, uncertain as to when another opportunity might offer, and for the same reasons I decided to accompany them: The captain, Sam Weller, came on shore to receive our money, and not one farthing less would he take.

The passengers were a poor and humble set. The food was indifferent, but the captain was a most attentive and first-rate seaman, and was never absent from his deck when his services were required. We sailed from the Cape about the end of April. My first night on board the Penyard Park was very miserable. I am six feet two inches, and could not stretch my legs, and was obliged to lie all doubled up in a most intensely uncomfortable position. I could not help complaining next morning. The captain said he was very sorry, but could not help me. At last a good-natured doctor said, "Well, Colonel Anderson, I'll see if I can help you." He then consulted his wife, and soon returned to say that, as his cabin was next to mine, he would order the carpenter to cut a hole through the partition above the level of his bed and raise my bed to that height, then to place over him a box long enough to receive my legs, and thus lengthen my bed as much as necessary. This novel mode of accommodation was soon completed by the carpenter, and from that day I was comparatively comfortable in my little cabin, and more than glad to hear that, although my box and my extra length were over the good doctor's legs every night during the voyage, he felt no inconvenience from the intrusion.

Chapter 16

Australia Once More

After a rather long and stormy passage we reached Sydney on the 4th June. An old servant of mine came on board at once, and from him I heard that my dear wife and children were all quite well and at Parramatta, so I at once wrote to her to announce my arrival, and promised to be with them in course of the day. I then hurried on shore and found a steamer starting for my home. There were many passengers on board who recognized me and who knew any wife, and from them I had the most delightful and cheering accounts of my family. Two anxious hours took us to Parramatta, and as we approached the wharf my house was pointed out to me on the opposite side of the river, and also my dear wife and children hurrying down to the bank to meet me, and my son Acland was seen by some of the passengers on the wharf waiting to greet me.

When he was pointed out to me I said, "Quite impossible—that cannot be my boy!" but before I had time to say another word he made a run, and a spring on to our deck, and in an instant was in my arms. My joy and delight were so great that for some seconds I could not speak. He was so grown, so handsome, well, and cheerful. It will be remembered I left him on his bed of sickness, most alarmingly ill; it was doubtful, indeed, if I should ever see him again. He then pointed out his mother and sisters anxiously waiting for us, so off we hurried. Our meeting was full of joy and thanksgiving. With the exception of my eldest daughter, Mary, I did not know one of them. So changed were they during the four years of my absence, that had I met them anywhere else I could not in any way have recognized them.

We went home and talked and talked, for we had much to say and no end of inquiries to make. Days and days passed before we became regularly composed and quietly settled down. I spent nearly a year with my wife and children, going occasionally to Sydney for a change, and to attend public and private parties and to dine at Government House. In December of that year my wife accompanied me in a steamer from Sydney to Melbourne for the purpose of visiting our station on the Goulburn River and determining whether it was advisable to settle down permanently in or near Melbourne. My health had by this time greatly improved, and I was getting over my lameness.

The long sea journey from Calcutta had done me much good, and I became stronger daily. We started from Melbourne in a gig for our station, Mangalore, and after four days' easy travelling got there early in January, 1846. My nephew, William Anderson, was then in charge. When we arrived there was no better accommodation than a common bark hut, with similar places at a little distance for the men; but the weather being fine and dry, we thought we could manage for a short time. My nephew did all he could to make us comfortable, and with our daily fresh meat and vegetables we fared very well. We took several drives in different parts of the station, and in a fortnight began our return journey to Melbourne. On our arrival there we took lodgings in Queen Street, intending to remain for some time and, if possible, to select some ground for our future residence.

Our inquiries for ground led me to make the acquaintance of a Mr. Archibald MacLaughlin, a wealthy merchant of Melbourne, who took us one morning to look at the land and site upon which my happy home, "Fairlie House," now stands, the adjoining land having been previously purchased by himself. The situation we at once thought beautiful, though then rough and without any house near it, or any signs or traces of the fine roads, streets, and houses which are now so near and all around it. However, after due consideration and visiting many other localities, I made up my mind to wait on his Honour Mr. La Trobe and request I might be allowed a special sale by auction of the land; he was the superintendent of the Port Phillip district, and subsequently lieutenant-governor of our colony of Victoria.

He received me very kindly, but said at once that he could not grant my request; that it was quite impossible that he could do so. I then spoke of my claims on the Government as an old officer and as the late superintendent for many years at Norfolk Island, but all to no purpose. He said he could not do it, and that he could make no distinction. I now remembered I had a letter from Mr. Deas Thompson, the Colonial Secretary at Sydney, expressing the readiness of the governor, Sir George Gipps, to assist me in every way in getting land in the Port Phillip district, as he understood I had thought of removing my family there. He read it, and, turning round, said with a smile, "Oh, this alters the question; I shall be glad to grant you a special sale by auction. Send me your application and name a day."

With this assurance I returned to my wife, and we agreed (as we had to return to Sydney) to leave all to Mr. MacLaughlin, and request him, as my agent, to send in the application and name a day for the sale. He kindly consented to do all this, and if successful at the sale to draw upon me for the amount. In a few days we left in the Shamrock steamer for Sydney, and after a pleasant passage were soon again with our children at Parramatta.

The next mail from England brought me my Order of the Bath and the long-expected War Medal with the four clasps for Maida, Talavera, Busaco, and Fuentes d'Onoro. This last gratifying distinction was for many long years objected to and opposed by the Duke of Wellington, but as often urged and recommended as a right and just acknowledgment by his late Royal Highness the Duke of York, and also by many peers and persons of distinction, for services in all parts of the world by the British army during the previous half-century. It was not till the year 1844 that the late Duke of Richmond brought the subject before the House of Lords, and, on his Grace's able showing, his motion was carried by a large majority, who recommended her Majesty to be pleased to grant to each regiment and corps her royal permission to bear on their colours and appointments the name of any victory in which they had been engaged since 1793, and for the officers and men to wear a silver medal suspended from a red ribbon with blue edge, and clasp thereon for every battle or action, showing the name of every such victory.

The officers of the army were so grateful to the Duke of Richmond for this service that committees were formed in London and in many of our principal towns in England, and in all foreign stations, for the purpose of getting up a subscription for a suitable testimonial in plate for his Grace, as a humble acknowledgment from the officers of the British army of the gratifying and very acceptable services he had rendered them. A large sum was collected, and a service of plate purchased and presented.

My next good news was a letter from Mr. MacLaughlin

stating that at the auction he had most fortunately been able to secure for me the land I had selected. We were indeed glad, as its position is delightful—overlooking the Botanical Gardens and the Government House domain, and with exquisite views of the bay on one side, and of Richmond, Kew, and the distant hills on the other. I at once wrote to my brother, who was in London, to send me the framework of a wooden house, on the plan of the Norfolk Island Government House, which he used to admire.

CHAPTER 17

Second Voyage to Calcutta

The period of my leave of absence was now drawing to a close. We received accounts from India of the campaign on the Sutlej and of the additional glory acquired by my gallant regiment in the battles of Moodkee, Ferozeshah, Aliwal, and Sobraon, and of all my dear friends who suffered or fell in those engagements. This made me more than ever anxious to be back with my regiment. In July of this year (1848) Captain Waddy and I made up our minds to take advantage of the first opportunity to secure our passages to India; soon afterwards we heard that the ship Mary Ann would sail for Calcutta in a few days with horses, and Captain Waddy engaged to make the necessary inquiries to secure our passages. In the meantime, after consulting with my wife and my son Acland (now in his sixteenth year), I determined to apply by memorial to the Commander-in-Chief at the Horse Guards for an ensigncy for my son. Captain Waddy secured our passages, and got himself appointed to take charge of the horses, with, of course, a number of grooms under him; by this he got free passages for himself and wife, and I believe the same allowance in money which any other person so employed would have received.

I took leave of my dear wife and children on the 6th August. I slept that night at the house of my cousin, Colonel James Gordon, who was then commanding the Royal

Engineers in Sydney, and embarked next day on the *Mary Ann*. We sailed for our destination, steering for the inward passage through Torres Straits. The weather was moderate and clear for the first ten days, and by this time we had passed Cape York and got well into the straits. The mainland at a distance and numerous small and large islands and rocks were constantly in sight, many of them very near. The wind was now fair, the captain and two men were constantly stationed on the fore top-sail yard, the former calling out to the men at the wheel "Port, starboard" or "Breakers ahead" or "Rocks on the lee bow" or "Port, starboard, steady!" and these were the constant warnings, almost every minute, daily. The lead was also kept going and the soundings reported, and at times a perfect silence ordered.

For days the navigation was most intricate. On one occasion we saw the masts of a schooner over a point of land; we steered round for her, and came to anchor near her. The captain asked me if I would accompany him in his boat to board her; I did so, and was a little surprised, after exchanging salutations, to find myself addressed by name by the captain, who said, "I hope Master Acland is quite well now." He told me he was from Sydney, and that my two dear boys were lodging with him when they were taken ill. This of course made me glad to meet him, to renew my thanks for his kindness to them. He was employed in the straits with his schooner, fishing for bêche-de-mer (or sea slugs) for the Chinese market. We left that anchorage the next morning, and after some hours' pleasant sailing got so near the mainland that we could see numbers of natives, who made signs to us, and we returned their salutation.

After this the weather got thick, with constant light rain for two or three days, and our progress became more perilous, and at times alarmingly dangerous. We could not see a hundred yards before us, and the captain had to depend entirely on his charts. On one of these trying days we reached a small island some hours before dark, and our captain prepared to bring up and anchor under the lee of it, but on getting there he could not find soundings. We then tried to get round as far as the wind would permit, but still found no bottom. He was obliged to give up all hope of coming to anchor, and could only carry on his course in the direction of the next island on his chart. He was visibly anxious, and so were we all, heavy rain still continuing and the night being unusually dark. It was indeed a black and dreadful night, and one of the most alarming I ever passed. We all kept on deck, no one went to bed, and I must confess I was afraid of going below, for I thought that if the worst happened we had a better chance of saving ourselves in the boats from the deck than if we remained below.

At about two next morning the captain thought he had run a sufficient distance to be pretty near the island for which he was steering, and he therefore brought the ship to the wind, intending to lie off till daylight. This was still an anxious time, for we had yet to wait some hours. At last the day dawned, and he found himself within a few miles of the island, at the very spot he believed himself to be in, and with the appearance of better weather, the rain and fog having cleared away.

We were indeed thankful, and soon forgot our troubles, for in two hours more we were seated at a good breakfast, as merry as ever, and our ship again on her course, running away from our island, with the sun shining once more brightly on us. In another week we arrived off Booby Island, the northern extremity of Torres Straits, thankful indeed for having got safely through that perilous voyage. The captain and Captain Waddy went on shore to the little island, taking with them, according to custom, a cask of water, a cask of salt beef, and a bag of biscuits; these were deposited in a cave in the rock called the "Post Office." It had been customary for years, for most vessels passing through the straits in safety, to leave some provisions at Booby Island, as a certain store and supply for shipwrecked sufferers, and, with humane feeling, this depot is always respected by visitors. It is named the "Post Office," as there is a large seaman's box there for letters, and also a book to insert the names of any vessels passing through, and the particulars of any losses or disasters occurring in the straits. Other ships passing take up these letters for delivery, according to their destination. Our people left letters at Booby Island, but one from me to my dear wife never reached her. She was more fortunate eighteen months later in receiving a letter left by our son Acland on his way to India.

I hope I shall never again go through Torres Straits, for it is not only a dangerous passage, but one which keeps one in constant alarm for three weeks or more. Some of the rocks seen in the direct course are not larger than a man's head over the water, others increasing to various sizes, and from the glare and rays of the sun, which are right ahead, they are not seen till one is within a few yards of them.

I have myself heard of several ships being wrecked going through the straits, and of one case where the whole of the passengers and crew fell into the hands of the natives, and were barbarously murdered and eaten, with the exception of one little boy, the son of a Captain and Mrs. D'Oyley—both of whom the unhappy child saw sacrificed with the others. He was rescued many months afterwards by Captain Lewis, of the colonial schooner Isabella, sent in search of the survivors by the Governor of New South Wales when news arrived in Sydney that the ship had never reached India, her destination. After many weeks' search amongst the islands, Captain Lewis got positive information from other natives that the ship was wrecked, and all on board, with the exception of one child, were murdered. He then made presents to these people, and got some of them to accompany him to the island where the massacre took place; there, through the efforts of his new friends and allies, he was kindly received, and after many more presents the boy was delivered up to him. He was also allowed to collect and carry away all the bones he could find of the unfortunate victims. These he brought to Sydney, where they were all buried together and a handsome monument placed over them.

Captain Lewis was allowed to take the survivor, little D'Oyley, home to England, to his nearest known relative; this he did at considerable inconvenience and expense. He soon discovered the grandfather, and delivered the boy to him, but instead of being handsomely rewarded for his services, he received nothing beyond expressions of many thanks, and as Captain Lewis was a poor man, depending entirely on his profession, all who knew him and this sad story were indignant, the more so as the boy's grandfather was known to be a man of considerable property.

Our detention at Booby Island was not long. We soon entered the Indian Ocean, and were steering for Copang, the capital of the Dutch island of Timor, and in three days we were safely anchored there. Our object was to fill water-casks for our horses, the consumption of water being great. Copang is an extensive, straggling, clean town, with a small fort and garrison of Dutch troops and a governor. For watering ships it is most convenient, the anchorage being within a few hundred yards of the shore, and the pure fresh water is carried in pipes to within a few yards of the beach and boats. We visited the governor and officers in the fort, who received us most kindly, and gave us coffee and cigars. We also spent many hours daily in a large shop or store, where all kinds of supplies could be purchased, and where the fat jolly Dutchman who kept it constantly treated us to coffee.

In a few days our tanks were full and all ready for sea, so we steered for the Bay of Bengal. The weather continued fine, and nothing remarkable occurred till our arrival off the Sand Heads. Then we received a pilot for Calcutta from one of the beautiful pilot-brigs which are constantly cruising off and on there. All was now excitement, getting scraps of news and preparing for the end of our long journey. We arrived about the middle of October, after a voyage. of three months. I had the satisfaction of receiving a packet of letters from my friend John Allan, inviting me to come at once to his house, and with the gratifying news that my boy Acland was appointed to an ensigncy in my own regiment, also that the 50th was then on its march from the upper Provinces, and actually under orders for England. All these unexpected changes were in consequence of the end of our war with the Sikhs. I landed the same evening, and was hospitably received by Mr. and Mrs. Allan.

Chapter 18

To Cawnpore and Back

Next day I reported my arrival to the adjutant-general, to the officer commanding at Calcutta, and officially to the officer commanding the 50th Regiment. I was next agreeably surprised by a visit from one of the officers, Major Tew, who informed me that Colonel Woodhouse was on his way down, and would soon be in Calcutta, and that they were both going to England on sick-leave. He gave me much interesting news of the regiment, and from him I heard for the first time of a regrettable incident which occurred before they left Loodhiana on their present march to Calcutta.

The regiment was quartered there when the Sutlej campaign commenced, and was suddenly ordered to join the army in the field at half an hour's notice. The officers were actually at their mess table when the order arrived, and they and their men were obliged to move at once, leaving the whole of their property, public and private, behind them, in charge of a guard; also the women and children and a few servants were left. The regiment was not gone many days when a large body of Sikhs marched into the town and to the military cantonments, and plundered, burnt, and destroyed almost everything there, not even sparing the officers' bungalows, many of which they either pulled down or burnt; and as they had no relish for the mess wines, they actually broke many dozens of full bottles. When the war was over the regiment returned to Loodhiana, and all were then apprised of their losses, which put them to serious inconvenience. They had not long returned before they were visited by a most violent gale, which in a few minutes levelled the men's barracks to the ground—a terrible calamity, as it buried beneath the ruins two hundred men, women, and children. About fifty of these were got out dead, the others more or less seriously wounded. To see so many brave soldiers, who had fought and escaped during the whole campaign, thus cruelly sacrificed was indeed truly heart-breaking.

I remained with my friend John Allan for more than a month. During that time I had many letters from the regiment, which kept me so well informed of their movements and march towards Calcutta that I saw no necessity to hurry my departure to meet them. An opportunity now offered direct for Sydney, and I gladly availed myself of it to write to my dear wife announcing my safe arrival. It was now the end of November, and finding that the regiment could not reach Calcutta before the beginning of March, I determined to join wherever I could most conveniently meet them on their march, and with this view took my passage early in December in one of the large and most comfortable river steamers for Allahabad. We were full of passengers for the upper Provinces, many of whom were very nice and agreeable.

Our voyage up the Hooghly and Ganges lasted upwards of a month. We often stopped for some hours at the principal towns and stations to land cargo and passengers, to coal, and to receive more goods and other passengers for the higher stations. The weather was beautiful, and I enjoyed the trip and the pleasant society very much. While we were at Dinapore another of the same steamers touched there, bound for Calcutta, and in her I had the pleasure of meeting Colonel Woodhouse on his way to England. He was not in good health. Of course we had much to say during our short interview. It was not till the 7th of January that we reached Allahabad, and there we all parted, after a very agreeable voyage.

I remained a few days at the hotel, and there found my old friends Sir Harry and Lady Smith, also on their way to England. I started in a small gharrie for Cawnpore, and there took quarters at an hotel, having heard that my regiment would arrive in two days more. On the following day the adjutant, Lieutenant Mullen, and Lieutenant Mowatt came in advance to welcome me, and to escort me to the regiment, and the next day we rode out to meet it. We had not proceeded more than three miles when we saw them approaching, and as soon as they recognized me they gave three cheers, and the band struck up "John Anderson, my joe." I took off my cap and returned their greeting with a fond and grateful heart, and again, as soon as I had reached the head of the column, three more cheers saluted me. Then Colonel Petit halted the regiment, to give me the opportunity of seeing and shaking hands with all the officers, and saying a few words to the men.

We now again got en route, and were met by Colonel Deare and many officers of the 21st Regiment and their band, who came from Cawnpore to welcome us, and so, surrounded by many hundreds of spectators, civil and military, we reached our camping-ground. No sooner had the Fusilier band taken up its position at our head than it struck up "See the Conquering Hero comes." Colonel Deare and his officers asked us to dinner, and the men of the 21st had our men in like manner to a general and merry feast. There was no end to our toasts and our fun. Colonel Petit handed me over the command of the regiment by a written order of that day. We continued our march the following morning, and in four days reached Benares, where we found a fleet of boats ready to receive us for Calcutta. I also found letters at the post-office, leaving to me the option of taking the passage from the Ganges to the Hooghly, or, if not practicable, to proceed through the more lengthy and tedious passage of the Sunderbunds (which are the numerous outlets of the mighty Ganges to the sea), from one of which there is a canal to the Hooghly at Calcutta.

We remained two or three days encamped near Benares, making our preparations and purchasing our private stock and provisions for the voyage. The commissariat having provided amply for our men, and all being ready, we started. The weather was fine, and all went on well till we arrived off the entrance of the Hooghly from the Ganges; there we brought up, and sent boats to see, and to sound, if there was a sufficient depth of water over the bar to carry our largest boats. They returned in a few hours, and reported that there was not sufficient water, and that we must take the passage through the Sunderbunds.

Next morning we started and steered accordingly, and brought up at the little village of Calpee, where it is the rule to take in pilots and provisions, and a sufficient quantity of fresh water to carry one through the Sunderbunds, as the water there is brackish half the way, and altogether salt afterwards. We found a resident magistrate at Calpee, and he furnished us at once with three pilots, and most kindly assisted us in getting provisions and many dozens of large earthen jars of fresh water. Being thus provided with a sufficient supply of all things needful for three or four weeks, we again proceeded on our voyage. One of the pilots was stationed with the advance guard, one with me as the commanding officer in the centre, and the third with the rear guard. All the boats of our fleet had strict orders to keep as much together as possible and not to lose sight of each other for a moment. As I said before, there are numerous and endless twists and turns, separate outlets and channels, in the Sunderbunds, and to take a wrong one is to take a risk of being lost altogether, and in a position from which one cannot extricate oneself to find the way back again to the proper course. To make sure, therefore, our best pilot was with the advance guard, and whenever he came to a fresh channel he halted till all our boats were in sight, and could distinctly see the change of our direction, then he again took the lead.

Buglers were in the boat of each pilot; these sounded the "Halt," "Advance," or "Close," according to circumstances, yet, notwithstanding all this precaution and care, we lost one of the boats, with soldiers and their families in it. We halted many days for them, and, fearing they might be short of provisions, I left a boat with supplies, as soon as we entered the last clear and certain course for Calcutta, with orders to come on if the missing boat did not appear in a week. Not only is the navigation difficult and dangerous, but the low lands and banks of the channels and creeks are covered with thick mangrove-trees and scrub, and we were assured by the pilot that it was infested in many places by tigers, ever ready to pounce upon any one within their reach.

CHAPTER 19

India to Cape Town

At last, after more than a fortnight's exposure to the pestilential atmosphere of the mangrove marshes and swamps, and repeated causes of uncertainty and anxiety about our proper course, we arrived early in March in the Hooghly, off Fort William, and landed in safety about an hour afterwards. We were no sooner formed in line than I observed an unusual appearance — a square of artillery of the right of the direct road to the fort; and on asking an officer what that was, he told me these were all the guns captured from the enemy during the various battles on the Sutlej. I instantly determined that my brave men should enjoy a near view of these trophies and proofs of their valour, so, instead of marching direct for the fort, I made a circuitous turn toward the guns, and then all round them.

The men were delighted, and their remarks were very amusing on pointing to many of the guns; for instance, "That is the fellow which knocked a whole section of ours to pieces!"; "That is the chap that knocked the colonel off his horse!"; and "Look, these are the very murdering devils which our charge settled and carried off at Aliwal!" The sight was really most gratifying, and truly calculated to inspire pride and glory in every British heart. There were in all upwards of three hundred guns of all sizes, from six to sixty-eight pounders, and principally brass, beautifully finished and mounted. After many cheers we marched into our barracks in Fort William. For the first ten days we had an increase of sick, but most of them recovered, though two or three poor men died. Our missing boat and the one left to pick it up both arrived in safety, about a fortnight after us; they were getting near the end of their provisions when they discovered their relief.

In Fort William we found the 16th Bengal Grenadiers, a regiment which wavered and held back to a man at the battle of Ferozeshah, leaving their English colonel to advance alone with our troops. He did all in his power to rally his men, but all to no purpose, so at last that brave man attached himself to our gallant 50th Regiment, and fought nobly with them, till, sad to say, he was at last killed.

Soon after our arrival at Calcutta we were asked to dinner by the Governor-General, Lord Hardinge. He was most kind to us all, and after dinner proposed the health of "Colonel Anderson and the officers of the 50th Regiment." He made a most brilliant and flattering speech, in which he enumerated most distinctly our services in all parts of the globe, and especially spoke of our indomitable and gallant conduct in the various battles of the Sutlej; then, turning to me, he said: "You may indeed, Colonel Anderson, be proud of your noble and distinguished regiment, and I have the most sincere pleasure in drinking your health, and the health and continued success of every officer and soldier of the brave 50th."

By this time I had heard much from my officers about the extent of their losses at Loodhiana, and I determined to make a strong appeal to the Government of India for remuneration. In due course I received an answer saying it was not customary for the Government to grant any indemnity for such losses, but that I might state the nature and particulars of the losses and amount in detail, for further consideration. I communicated the answer to the officers, and requested them to furnish me with a detailed account of all their losses. When it was all complete I forwarded it to the Secretary of the Military Department, and begged that it might be favourably considered. A long time passed without my receiving an answer; but ; at last I got a letter informing me that the demands were unreasonable, that the officers had no claim or right to such expensive bungalows, that they should have been built in value according to their relative ranks, and that the officers' mess should not have had such costly wines.

To this I replied that the comfort and health of the officers was of the first importance to the efficiency of the service, that the additional accommodation tended to their comfort and good; and with respect to the expensive and large stock of our mess wines, I said such was the custom of all officers' messes in the regiments of her Majesty's Service, and more especially in India, where the carriage was so expensive, and where the messes of British officers were expected to entertain in suitable and becoming manner, which duty they could not carry out if their supplies of wine were limited.

To this I received a reply that the Government of India could not, after due consideration, grant any remuneration for the losses without establishing a precedent which must be inconvenient hereafter. I wrote once more, saying that I still ventured to make one more appeal in so just and good a cause, and stated that the officers interested were seriously inconvenienced by their losses, and by the very unexpected decision of the Government, and consequently that I considered it my imperative duty to request that the subject might be reconsidered. In another week I got an answer granting all we claimed, with the exception of a reasonable deduction from the value the officers had placed on their expensive bungalows. This then was a great victory, and my officers were indeed glad and thankful for the service I had rendered them.

Early in January, 1848, I received an order to hold the regiment in readiness for embarkation, and I was at the same time informed that one-third of the officers would be permitted to proceed home at once by the overland route, at the public expense, if they preferred it. The selection was left to me, and I was directed to forward the names at once to the Adjutant-General of her Majesty's Forces in India, that their leave of absence might appear in General Orders. Accordingly, I saw the necessity of keeping most of the senior officers to take charge of and accompany their men during the long voyage, and was happy to find that many had no particular wish to go overland.

I therefore soon made my selection without disappointing any one, and amongst the number I included my own dear son. The names of the chosen few were forwarded, and in due time appeared in General Orders, with three months' leave of absence. This liberal time was given to afford them an opportunity of visiting any other parts of Europe and Asia beyond the immediate line of route. In a few days the mail steamer for Suez started, and they went off with light hearts. The arrangements and terms of the mail steamer were most liberal, for they allowed passengers to leave them at any of the ports of call for a month or six weeks, and took them up again at the same place without additional charge.

About the middle of January three splendid ships were placed at my disposal for the conveyance of my regiment to England, viz., the Queen, Marlborough, and Sutlej. They were all of the largest class, and, after visiting and inspecting each, I could not make up my mind which I should prefer for mine as headquarters. They were all equally tempting, and the accommodation in all most inviting and comfortable. At last I decided on the Queen for headquarters, and for three companies, and ordered the remainder of the regiment to be divided between the Marlborough and Sutlej, the former under the command of Captain Bonham, the latter under Major Long. In the last week in January the embarkation took place. The Sutlej took the lead, and the Marlborough followed next day, and on the morning of the 3rd February I embarked, thankful indeed to leave a land and climate which I always disliked, and with an anxious hope that I might never be doomed to visit it again.

We all were comfortable and happy on board, and our table was most amply and liberally provided. In addition to my officers we had a number of passengers, and as we had our band with us, we had music and dancing every evening. During the first three weeks the weather was very favourable, then fresh breezes and contrary winds followed occasionally, but nothing to disturb or distress us. About the middle of April we made the Cape of Good Hope, and as we approached Cape Town we were joined by, and came up with, a number of other ships, all steering for the anchorage at Table Bay. One of these in the distance appeared under three jury-masts, and to our surprise she proved to be one of our own ships, the Sutlej.

We were now all anxiety to know the cause of her mishap and the extent of her damages and loss, fearing that some of our men must have suffered much during so serious a misfortune; but we were obliged to wait till both ships got to anchor. Then our captain and some of our officers went on board the Sutlej, and on their return to us reported that on the night of the 1st of April they had met a severe gale, which suddenly carried away the three masts by the deck, but fortunately without injuring any one, beyond a few bruises. They all had a most providential escape.

The sea was running mountains high, and when the masts fell over the side and were being cut away clear of the hull, the end of one of them was forced through one of the dead-lights in the stern, which at once admitted the sea in tons, to a most fearful and alarming extent, and so continued for some minutes, till stopped by mattresses and some other temporary contrivances, and the pumps and dozens of buckets were kept going all the time. I was assured that even with all these precautions and means they must have foundered but for the able and willing assistance the captain and crew received from our gallant soldiers on board, for the former were all but exhausted with the previous fatigues of the gale, and the soldiers were fresh and ever ready to assist and lend a hand.

General Cartwright of the Bengal army and Major Mackay of the 21st were passengers on board, both so seriously ill that they could not leave their cabins during the disaster, and the former had a narrow escape of his life, his illness being much increased by one of the top-masts actually falling through the deck into his cabin, but fortunately clear of his bed.

CHAPTER 20

Return to England

Soon after we had anchored, I landed to report our arrival, and found to my great pleasure that our old friend Sir Harry Smith commanded at the Cape. He was very glad to see us, and at once determined to land the whole of our detachment from the Sutlej, as the ship would require new masts and thorough repairs, which would take many weeks to carry out. They were disembarked and accommodated in barracks next morning, and on that day we all dined with Sir Harry and Lady Smith. Neither of our ships had seen our other vessel, the Marlborough, since the day she left us at Calcutta. We in the *Queen* remained in Table Bay for a week, and continued to receive the greatest kindness and hospitality from Sir Harry Smith.

We then left and steered for St. Helena, which was reached in about ten days. We anchored there three days, and the officers were allowed to land daily if they wished. Finally we made all sail for England, without anything remarkable beyond calms and contrary winds, in consequence of which we had rather a long passage. We had no sickness on board, and our evening musical parties and dancing were continued. About the end of May we sighted the happy land of England, and on the 1st of June were off the Isle of Wight; on the morning of the 3rd we passed Deal, and there saw our good ship the Marlborough at anchor and without any troops on board, so we concluded at once that our detachment from that ship had landed. This was soon confirmed by a boat which boarded us and told us that they had disembarked some days before at Deal, where the depot of the regiment was stationed.

Our captain continued his course according to instructions, and on the 4th of June we anchored off Gravesend; and now all was excitement and preparation for landing, and by that day's post I reported our arrival to the Adjutant-General of her Majesty's Forces at the Horse Guards. Early next day we were boarded by a staff officer from Tilbury Fort; he informed me he expected the order every minute for our landing, and requested me to prepare accordingly. We were soon all ready, and the order for our disembarkation and route for the barracks in Chatham soon came.

Boats were immediately alongside, and in less than an hour the 50th Regiment was again drawn up on English ground, with the shattered but proud remains of our colours flying over us, and behind them three large new embroidered Sikh colours captured by the regiment in the battles of the Sutlej, and now the glorious trophies of our valour and renown. These, and the well-known character of the "Fighting 50th," caused great excitement and a general gathering of the inhabitants of Gravesend.

There was no end to the cheering and welcomes which greeted us, and in this way the mass of the crowd followed us nearly to Chatham, and there we were received with similar honours by the commandant and all the officers and soldiers of the garrison. We dined with the officers of the garrison, and our men were feasted, and made much of by the soldiers of the different depots. Next morning we marched for Canterbury, where we halted and dined with the 21st Regiment, and went on by rail next morning to Deal, where we were met by many of our depot officers and men, and amongst the former my own dear son. We marched to our barracks and spent a very happy evening.

I had last seen my son, on board the mail steamer at Calcutta, starting for England. I now learnt from him that he and his companions had stopped a few days at Cairo, and also at Alexandria, and then went on to Malta, where they remained some days. They next took their passage in a steamer for Civita Vecchia, thence by diligence on to Rome; they then went to Marseilles, and thence to Paris. Before they were many days in the gay capital of France, the Revolution suddenly broke out in all its horrors, and they managed by stratagem to escape from Paris, and to make their way with others to Havre, where they at once embarked for England — thankful, indeed, that they had got away with their lives, without either wounds or broken bones, considering they were for a time under fire and exposed to the risk of death. In their hurry to get away they were obliged to leave most of their clothing and baggage behind.

I was now expecting to be relieved from the command of the regiment. Colonel Woodhouse was still absent on leave, but was expected to join shortly. In another week I received an official letter informing me that I and our supernumerary lieutenants (six) would be placed on half-pay in a month from that date. This we expected, and I endeavoured to bear it in the hope of better luck, and that I might again be employed on full pay some future day — but I determined to stay with my dear regiment till Colonel Woodhouse joined. I had not to remain long, for in another week he was with us, and I, of course, handed the command over to him. Poor man, he was in bad health, and was confined to his house and could see no one. He was still commanding officer, and the adjutant carried on all details in his name. I remained packing up and preparing for my final departure, then took leave of my friends, little expecting to see them or the regiment again, and started for London.

Some days afterwards I attended the Adjutant-General's levee at the Horse Guards. He received me most kindly. After asking a few questions about the regiment and our voyage, he suddenly said, "Would you, Colonel Anderson, like to be employed again?" My answer was ready, that most certainly I should. "Have you been with Lord Fitzroy Somerset?" he asked (the Commander-in-Chief and Military Secretary). I replied that I had not. On which he said, "You sit here, and I will see him at once." He soon returned, and told me he could not see him then, as the Duke of Cambridge was with him, but added he would take an early opportunity of seeing Lord Fitzroy about me. Shortly after this Colonel Woodhouse retired. We all greatly regretted his loss. He had been nearly forty years in the regiment, and had commanded it for twenty-five years.

I attended Lord Fitzroy Somerset's next levee. He received me very kindly, and I mentioned my desire to be again employed. His lordship replied, "Very well, Colonel Anderson, I will make a note of it; but you had better write to me and state your wishes." He made no allusion whatever to Colonel Woodhouse, nor did I. Next day I wrote to his lordship officially, merely requesting that I might be again employed. I was some days without an answer, but I was not kept very long in suspense ere I received a letter ordering me to proceed at once to Deal, to resume the command of the 50th Regiment. This was great and glorious news, and all that my heart could desire. Next day I arrived at Deal, and was received most kindly by all. Colonel Petit handed me over the command, and I was once more at the head of my dear regiment. Colonel Petit handed me over, amongst other official papers, a letter from the

Adjutant-General intimating that Colonel Woodhouse was placed on half-pay, and Lieut.-Colonel Anderson ordered to rejoin and take command of the regiment. From this time all went well, but we had all enough hard work in distributing our depot men amongst our battalion companies, preparing our new clothing, and drilling and exercising morning and evening and making everything ready for our next general inspection. About the end of July we heard of the arrival of the Sutlej off Gravesend, with Major Long's detachment, and in a few days they were with us. Our colonel-in-chief, General Sir George Gardner, paid us a visit about this time, and made a general inspection of the regiment. He was considered a very able and strict officer. He now made a minute inspection, and after seeing us go through various movements, he closely inspected our interior arrangements and economy, and finally expressed himself well pleased.

Chapter 21
Farewell to the 50th Regiment

I now heard from my wife in answer to my last letter, in which I urged her to make such arrangements for the safety and management of our property in Victoria and Melbourne as might enable her at once to return to England, and so join me. Her answer was full of good sense, saying she could not make up her mind to trust any one she knew with the entire care and management of our property; that the risk and chances of loss were too great for her to take the whole responsibility of appointing any one to act for us, and therefore, however sad our continued separation must be to us both, she considered it wise and prudent to remain where she was till she heard further from me; and I could not but concur in the wisdom of this opinion.

Having long and well considered our relative situations and the discomforts and distress which we must endure by a continued separation, I now began for the first time to think seriously about retiring from the service by the sale of my commission, and returning to my family in Australia for the rest of my life. These were serious and most trying thoughts, and not to be carried out in a hurry. To think of leaving my dear regiment for ever, and the service, to which no man was ever more devoted, and in which I had spent nearly the whole of my life, was most agonizing, and I could scarcely endure it.

At last we marched to Dover, and on the way I got into conversation with Major Petit, then the senior major of the regiment and the first for purchase. After much friendly talk I hinted to him that I would not mind retiring if I was offered a good price above the regulations. At once he asked me how much I would expect. I did not then give him any answer beyond saying I would think about it. I did think about it again and again, but I could not make up my mind, not that I hesitated about the additional sum I would ask, but about going or not going. This was towards the end of August, and I was then called on by a very dear friend, Captain Dodd, who told me he was requested by Colonel Petit and the next officers in succession for purchase to ask if I really had serious thoughts of retiring, and, if so, what additional sum I would expect. I told Captain Dodd that I had thought about it, but could not make up my mind. As I have said, he was a dear friend of mine, and we now talked long on the subject, which ended by his telling me he thought he could get them to make an additional sum of fifteen hundred pounds above the regulation. Finally I promised to make up my mind and give my final decision in a few days.

This fearful state of suspense and anxiety began to disturb my general health, and it became so bad that I could not attend parade or even leave my rooms. The surgeon attended me all this time, and recommended me to go on leave of absence, as I required a change, and it would certainly do me good. I was granted two months' sick-leave, and I promised Colonel Petit that he should have my final and positive answer in a week. In ten days' time I was really quite resigned when I saw myself gazetted out of the service, and my friend Petit and the others promoted in succession. This was a relief and great satisfaction to me, as it at once removed the anxiety I felt about them, for I sometimes doubted whether the succession and promotion would go in the regiment. A few days more brought me a letter from Colonel Petit informing me that he had instructed our agents, Messrs. Cox & Co., to place fifteen hundred pounds (beyond the regulation) to my credit, these sums making in all six thousand pounds for my commission, and so ended (on the 28th of September, 1848) my services as a soldier.

The die was cast, the deed was done and could not be recalled, and I was indeed utterly unhappy and miserable. For forty-three years I had served my Sovereign faithfully. My whole mind and heart were devoted to my profession. I had risked my health and life in several countries and in battlefields often and often, and these memoirs show the extent of favour and success which repeatedly attended my humble endeavours.

All that was now left to me was the fond remembrance of the past and the conviction that I had still, and ever would have, the heart of a soldier, and I hoped to be able to pass the remainder of my eventful life in peace and thankfulness with my dear wife and children. I must here mention such was the state of my health at this time that I had great fear that I should not live long enough to see them. But God was good and more merciful to me than I deserved; for His mercy not only restored me to them in due time, but He has granted me ever since to this day many, many of the most happy, and I may also say most healthy, years of my long life, and I am indeed thankful.

A Brief History of Anderson's Campaigns

by Eric Sheppard

Publisher's Note

The following passages from Eric Sheppard's book *A Short History of the British Army to 1914* provide background and context to Anderson's time in India.

The Leonaur Editors

The British Conquest of Bengal

Bengal in the year 1758 had the puppet Meer Jaffier as its nominal ruler, subject in theory to the overlordship of the *faineant* Mogul Emperor in Delhi, in practice to the dictates of Clive and the East India Company's representatives at Calcutta. But in the nature of things this state of affairs could only be of short duration. In the next seven years the land became an acknowledged portion of British territory—the first province of British India.

The Mogul Emperor, Shah Alam, unwilling tamely to reconcile himself to seeing Bengal slip from his control, enlisted the help of Shuja ud Dowlah, the ruler of Oude, the province bordering its western frontier, and early in 1760 marched to recover his lost possession. The British contingent, serving as an auxiliary force to Meer Jaffier's army, numbered only some 1500 men, under the command of Caillaud; but it was entirely thanks to it that the first advance of the Allies against Patna met with a decided repulse at Seerpore, the part played by the Bengalis themselves being inglorious in the extreme. The Emperor in actual fact reaped all the fruits of the battle; moving round his adversaries' left, he effected a vigorous foray which compelled them to fall back hastily in order to cover Moorshedabad, their capital, and then, returning on his tracks, invested Patna, weakly garrisoned and already menaced by a French auxiliary corps under Law. At the last moment his prey was snatched from his grasp by the arrival of a small British column under Knox, which had marched 300 miles in the space of thirteen days to the rescue of the beleaguered city; the siege was raised and the Allies retired southwards, leaving Knox free to deal at his leisure with the Nawab of Purneah, who, advancing on the north bank of the Ganges to complete the investment, was vigorously assailed and routed in a hotly contested action at Beerpore. Meanwhile the main British army, under a new commander, Carnac, had reached Patna, and, following up Shah Alam and his confederate in their retirement towards Behar, inflicted on him a smart defeat which forced him to sue for terms. One of the conditions laid upon him was that he should install Meer Kossim as Nawab of Bengal in place of the aged and incapable Meer Jaffier, who went into reluctant retirement at Calcutta.

The energy and ability of the new ruler, however advantageous to his subjects, who for the first time for many years found themselves well and justly governed, soon brought him into open conflict with the East India Company and its servants, who regarded Bengal only as a sponge to be squeezed and its ruler as a convenient tool to effect such squeezing. Here, fortunately, we are concerned only with the military phase of this, perhaps the most discreditable chapter in the history of British India. Early in 1763, Meer Kossim, who had at his disposal a well-organised and trained force of some 45,000 men, and had obtained the assistance of the Emperor in his quarrel, was at open war with the Company, whose available troops numbered barely 11,500 in all. Hostilities opened with a serious disaster to the British. A treacherous and unprovoked attack made by them on Patna miscarried owing to the indiscipline of the troops, and while endeavouring to retreat they were overtaken and surrounded in open country and compelled to lay down their arms to the number of 3000 men. It was under these unfavourable auspices that Adams, at the head of a little force of 2500 men, commenced his advance up the Ganges from Calcutta. Meer Kossim's advance guard was heavily defeated in an attempt to cover Moorshedabad, and Adams, his troops doubled in numbers soon after the occupation of that city, found himself face to face with 40,000 enemy troops in a strong position at Sooty. After a desperate day's fighting the defence was broken through and fell back to the defile of Oondwa, where a marsh and powerful entrenchments closed the narrow gap between river and hills. For a whole month the British force was held up before this formidable obstacle; then in a daring and skilfully conducted night operation a path through the marsh was threaded, the fortifications were stormed and the troops of Meer Kossim were driven out with the loss of all their guns and several thousand men. Four weeks later trenches were opened before the walls of Patna, the storming of which put an end to the operations. Meer Kossim, defeated and desperate, sought refuge in Oude, and Carnac replaced Adams, who retired to Calcutta, sick to death, after a campaign which, for audacity and brilliance, will bear comparison with any recorded in the military history of India.

The new British General, who was made of less heroic stuff than his predecessor, found himself, at the opening of the campaign of 1764, faced with the forces not only of the two princes who had gone down before Adams, but also with those of the Nawab of Oude, while the European portion of his own army was discontented and inclined to be mutinous. Compelled to a hasty and somewhat undignified withdrawal within the walls of Patna, he nevertheless succeeded in maintaining himself there long enough to allow time for discord to arise among his adversaries, who, following the failure of their first assault on the city, retired to Buxar. Here Meer Kossim, broken and disgraced, finally disappeared from the scene, and his former allies sat down to fortify their lines and await the attack of the British army, now once more under a worthy leader, Hector Munro.

The latter, after repressing an outbreak of serious disaffection among his native troops, moved on Buxar with 7000 men to encounter the overwhelmingly superior forces of the Emperor and the Nawab, variously estimated at from 40,000 to 60,000. On October 23, 1764, he found them drawn up outside their entrenchments to give him battle. In the ensuing encounter Munro both outmanoeuvred and outfought his opponents; their left wing, after fierce fighting, was driven in on their centre, broken into fragments and hurled back with fearful carnage into the muddy bed of a stream, which was only passed by the survivors over a bridge of their comrades' corpses. 847 British casualties were the price of this decisive victory; 2000 enemy dead and 167 captured guns its trophies. The conquerors pushed forward rapidly to Benares and beyond it to Allahabad, and here, well within the territory of Oude, dictated their terms of peace, which included the recognition by the Emperor of the full practical sovereignty of the East India Company over Bengal, Behar and Orissa, and an offensive and defensive alliance of the late belligerents.

From whatever point of view it be regarded, Buxar has an undeniable claim to rank as a decisive battle in the history of India, of Great Britain and of the world; yet its name is unknown to the average educated man, so true is it that personalities rank in popular estimation more highly than achievements. It is because Clive was one of the greatest Englishmen of his day, and Munro merely an able soldier, that the military promenade of Plassey is remembered and the hard-fought victory of Buxar forgotten; yet the results of the latter, marking as they do the first definite stepping-stone to the achievement of British supremacy in India, far surpassed those of the former, and Hector Munro well merits at least a niche in the Pantheon of our Empire-builders.

The heroic deeds of toe Bengal army in the field were followed by a curious anti-climax in the shape of a strike among the commissioned ranks, secretly backed up by certain malcontent civilian elements, for the maintenance in peace time of their none too munificent war-time rates of pay. Clive, who had returned from England, after having well feathered his own nest, with full powers to deal drastically with corruption in Bengal wherever found, repressed this movement with the energy of a poacher turned gamekeeper; and having successfully accomplished this task, turned to the more fruitful one of reorganising the army, which was now redistributed into three brigades, each of one European and seven Sepoy battalions, with a total establishment of 17,000 of all ranks.

With the exception of the Rohilla War, where a force co-operated with the troops of Oude and distinguished itself greatly at the action of Babul, no military operations of any importance took place in Bengal for the next forty years.

The Second Mahratta War

The overthrow of the power of Mysore in 1800 left the East India Company, supreme in the south and east of the Peninsula, face to face with the extensive domain of the Mahratta Confederacy, extending over the whole of Central and Northern India, from the Himalayas south and beyond the Kistna, and from Cuttack on the shores of the Bay of Bengal westwards to Gujerat. A fierce and warlike people, whose roving horsemen had spread the terror of their name far beyond their own boundaries, they bade fair to be worthy foemen even for the victors of Buxar and Porto Novo, while their possession of Delhi and its impotent puppet ruler, who still personified for the mass of the Indian people the legendary empire of the Moguls, seemed to give them a prescriptive legal right to inherit the power which they in fact exercised in his name. Fortunately for the British, neither to Shah Alam nor to any supreme chief even of their own race did the Mahrattas owe any but nominal allegiance; they were in fact no more than a loose confederacy of independent chieftains, incapable of long pursuing any coherent policy, divided by mutual jealousies and inherited rivalries, formidable when united in arms, but seldom so united for long. Blind to their own true interests, they had, as we have already seen, neglected to take advantage of England's difficulties and perils during her long struggle with Mysore, and so lost their best chance of crushing at birth the growing power of the intruders; and when they were themselves in turn assailed by the conquerors of Hyder and Tippoo, they refused to sink their mutual; differences even before the prime necessity of opposing a united front to the common enemy.

In fact, while Lord Wellesley and his Generals were methodically completing the overthrow of Tippoo, the Mahrattas were wasting their energies in a fierce internecine strife. The death in 1793 of Mahadaji Sindia removed from the scene the one statesman who had fully realised the extent of the British menace, and consistently striven to unite the whole confederacy to meet it; his successor, the incapable Daulat Rao, fell out with two of his brother chieftains, Baji Rao, the Peshwa who aimed at the recovery of the supremacy which had always been exercised by his house, in theory at least, over all the Mahratta dominions, and Jeswant Rao Holkar, who played now and throughout his life simply for his own hand. Fighting broke out and continued with many vicissitudes of fortune until in 1802 fortune turned decisively against the Peshwa, who in desperation sought refuge in Bombay territory and implored British aid in the recovery of his dominions. This he obtained, and was triumphantly escorted back to his capital of Poona, under the terms of the Treaty of Bassein—a signal diplomatic triumph for the British, who by it accentuated the split in the Mahratta camp, and secured without fighting, not only an entry into the Peshwa's territory, but a right to interfere in the internal affairs of the confederacy. Now, at length, the warring chiefs realised to the full the danger which so nearly menaced them. Daulat Rao Sindia, the ruler of the whole vast belt of land from the northern frontier of Hyderabad on the Godavery northward to Delhi and the Himalayan foothills, began to make ready his army for war against the British, and summoned to his aid Ragoji Bhonsla of Berar, whose territories extended from Nagpore on the west to Cuttack on the Bay of Bengal. The forces which those two chiefs could put into the field amounted in all to close on 100,000 men, among whom, in addition to the famous cavalry, there were a number of battalions and batteries armed and trained on European lines and led by French soldiers of fortune. Jeswant Rao Holkar, however, in an evil hour for his race and himself, resolved to pursue his traditional policy of selfish isolation and refused for the present to declare against the British.

During the period of long-drawn-out and insincere negotiations which extended from May to August 1803, the British armies were mustered for the war that the Governor-General saw to be inevitable. The plan of campaign consisted of a double attack on Sindia in the north and the south, combined with subsidiary operations against Bundelcund, Cuttack and Gujerat on the left flank of each of these main offensives. Of the northern operations, including those against Bundelcund and Cuttack, Lord Lake, the Commander-in-Chief, was in personal charge, with a force of 21,000 men, of whom 6000 were allotted to the former attack and 5000 to the latter theatre, leaving 10,000 for the main army. Arthur Wellesley, the Governor-General's brother, whose later career in Europe we have recently followed to its apotheosis at Waterloo, was in command in the south, having general control of the operations of his own army of 11,000 men, the Hyderabad contingent of 9000 under Stevenson, which was to co-operate with him in the main offensive, and Murray's 4000, whose mission it was to occupy Gujerat—and who, it may here be said, to save further reference to this force, succeeded in doing so with little difficulty.

In August 1803, Arthur Wellesley, realising that nothing was to be hoped for from further conversations with Sindia and the Bhonsla, exercised the discretionary power given him and moved forward from his area of concentration east of Poona against the strongly fortified little place of Ahmednagar, which he at once stormed out of hand and made his advanced base. Stevenson had meanwhile crossed the Hyderabad frontier, and the two armies effected their junction at Aurungabad. The enemy, who, to the strength of some 50,000 men, had been assembling north of the Ajunta hills, now in their turn took the offensive in the direction of Hyderabad territory, but being headed off by Wellesley, fell back slowly northwards, and were overtaken and brought to battle at Assaye. The British General, though his forces were so split up that he could only bring some 6000 men on to the field, boldly assailed the hostile left, and after fierce fighting drove them from their ground with heavy loss, practically all Sindia's infantry being destroyed; the remnant fled in disorder beyond the Tapti, followed by Stevenson, who had taken no part in the battle. While the latter was besieging and taking the fortress of Asirgarh, Wellesley, who was refitting his army and collecting supplies at Aurungabad for a renewed offensive, was once more called on to deal with incursions by the Mahratta cavalry, who endeavoured to sweep round his left and rear to harry the country south of the Godavery. Before long, however, he was ready to resume his advance, which was directed against the Bhonsla's capital of Nagpore; Ragoji, attempting to oppose his progress, was swept aside at Argaum, and the capture by storm of the hill fortress of Gawilgarh left his territory at the mercy of the British. But before Wellesley could crown his brilliant campaign by the occupation of his opponent's capital, the latter, his spirit broken by the evil news from the north, sued humbly for terms.

Lake's campaign had been even more rapid and decisive than that of his famous lieutenant. Assembling his army of 10,000 men at Cawnpore, he set out up the Ganges and the Kali at the end of July, invested Aligarh, reputed to be one of the strongest fortresses in India, broke his way in through a series of strongly defended gates and practically annihilated the garrison. Thence he pursued his way towards Delhi, outside which city he came upon Sindia's main army, close on 20,000 men, entrenched for battle, whereas he himself had less than 5000 available. Drawing the enemy from their positions by a feigned retirement of his cavalry, he drove them from the-field by one deadly volley and a bayonet charge, and pushing on entered Shah Alam's capital city, to be hailed as a deliverer by the aged and blinded Emperor. Crossing to the west bank of the Jumna, he then marched south to Agra, where he came on part of the beaten Mahratta army standing to fight on the glacis of the place. Having attacked and driven them off to the west, he delayed a few days to get possession of the fort, and then set off once more on the trail of his adversaries, who had now been reduced by losses and desertion to a residue of some 14,000 men only. A march of portentous length and rapidity brought the British up with their foes at Laswari, and there was fought out on November 1 the most hotly contested and desperate battle hitherto recorded in the history of our army in India. For some time the fate of the day hung by a thread, but at length the Mahratta right was turned and broken, and their host completely destroyed or dispersed. It needed only the loss of Sindia's capital of Gwalior to complete the ruin of his fortunes, and he too was not slow to follow the example of his ally and sue for peace, which was concluded in December 1803. The British gains by the treaty were great and important, including as they did the territories of Bundelcund and Cuttack, which had fallen into their hands with little resistance soon after the outbreak of war, and all Sindia's and the Bhonsla's lands east of the Jumna and south of the Tapti.

But the task of the British, though well begun, was little more than half done as yet. Scarcely four months had passed before Jeswant Rao Holkar, resolved to try his fortune where his rivals had failed, threw down the gage in his turn, and in April 1804 Lake and his troops took the field once more against this new enemy. Holkar had learnt at least one lesson from the Mahratta defeats of the previous year, and resolved to rely for his own part no longer on artillery and infantry, who could too easily be brought to battle and beaten, but on the mobility of his masses of horsemen. Driven by Lake's advance from his first position near Jaipur, he withdrew southwards across the Chambal, leaving the fortified town of Rampura to be invested and taken by his enemies. The hot weather being now well come, the British General deemed it impracticable to keep all his forces in the field and withdrew his main body to Agra, entrusting the observation and pursuit of Holkar to a force of 4000 men under Monson, with whom Murray from Gujerat in the south was to co-operate by an advance on Indore. The latter, however, whose military incapacity we have already learnt to know at Tarragona, failed to perform his part in the combined scheme, thus leaving all the Mahratta army free to deal with Monson, who was compelled by the pressure of immensely superior forces to a disastrous retreat of 250 miles over flooded rivers and swampy plains; all his guns and baggage had to be abandoned, and less than half his detachment eventually escaped to Agra in the last stages of exhaustion and demoralisation.

Holkar's triumph, though great and resounding, was short-lived; for the indefatigable Lake was at once at hand to restore the situation. While half the Mahratta army swung north to recover Delhi and the remainder menaced Agra to cover their movement, the British forces were being assembled for the counter-offensive at Muttra. As soon as Lake realised the situation, he pushed from his path the enemy detachment in his immediate front and hurried northward to Delhi. The garrison of that city, under the able direction of Ochterlony, though only 2500 strong, successfully held their tenfold superior assailants at bay until the sound of Lake's guns on his rear compelled Holkar hurriedly to raise the siege and flee up the west bank of the Jumna. The British horse followed hard after him, having dropped their infantry under Fraser to deal with the Mahratta force which had remained before Agra. The Mahratta chief, turning sharp to east and south near Meerut, made his way at full speed down the Kali, reached the Ganges valley at Farrukabad and, knowing Lake to be well in rear, halted for a breathing space. But he had underestimated the energy and driving power of his pursuer; covering 70 miles in 24 hours, the British burst into his camp at dawn and scattered its occupants to the four winds. Holkar himself with a few followers alone escaped from the massacre.

Fraser's operations had been equally successful, and the enemy force in his front encountered in a strong position, backed on the fortress of Deig, had been driven to seek refuge within its walls. Lake, returning from his chase of Holkar, ordered the place to be invested and stormed, which was accordingly done; and the army, flushed with victory, proceeded to lay siege to the capital of the Jat Rajah of Bhurtpore, a former friend of the British, who had turned against them after Monson's disaster. Here, however, its victorious career received a decided setback. The fortress was large and immensely strong; Lake's artillery was hopelessly inadequate to deal with its defences; and Holkar, with the remnant of his rallied troops, was hovering in the vicinity to harry and distract the attention of the besiegers. No less than four large-scale assaults were delivered during the course of the siege, which lasted from January to April 1815, and were beaten off with severe loss, and at length Lake was compelled to draw off his baffled troops. The blow to British prestige was more important than the immediate results of the failure, for the Rajah at once made his peace with Lake and set the latter free once more to deal with Holkar. Part of the Mahratta horse, detached to raid Lake's line of communications during the siege, had been driven eastward into Rohilcund and there defeated and dispersed, so that the residue amounted to barely 8000 men, and their leader's efforts to induce Sindia to unite with him for a final effort against the British failed before the menace of Lake's renewed advance. He therefore retreated to Ajmeer and thence northward to the Sutlej, hoping in vain to get help from the Sikhs. Lake followed him up and drove him to seek refuge in Punjab territory, where, in December 1805, the last shots of the war were fired.

Unhappily the fruits of this decisive shattering of the Mahratta power by the overthrow in succession of all their greatest chieftains were sacrificed at the conclusion of peace in January 1806. The Directors of the East India Company, alarmed at the peril and cost of Lord Wellesley's aggressive policy, had sent put Cornwallis to replace him; and on the latter's death after a few weeks in the country Barlow was appointed Governor-General with instructions to end the war at all costs and refrain from further acquisitions of territory. Accordingly Holkar found to his astonishment all his former possessions restored to him, and, what was worse, liberty to wreak his vengeance on many of his vassals who had adhered to the British cause during the war. The Mahratta power was thus scotched indeed, but not killed; for that another and even greater war was to be necessary.

None the less, the major part of the work had been accomplished by Arthur Wellesley and Lake. Of the former, whose character and career we have already discussed, it is enough to say here that he had shown himself as much a master of Eastern as later of Western warfare. His colleague and commander in these campaigns displayed qualities at least as pre-eminent— brilliant leadership in battle, tireless and all-conquering energy in advance and pursuit, an unsurpassed power of getting the best out of his officers and men, and a complete and chivalrous loyalty to inferiors and superiors alike. Of all the galaxy of great leaders who gained their fame on Indian fields, Lake's is one of the outstanding and most attractive figures.

The Nepal Campaign and the Overthrow of the Mahratta Confederacy

For some years after the sacrifice of Lord Wellesley's gains at the behest of the East India Company's directors at home, Barlow and his successor, Lord Minto, were able to carry out the policy laid down for them by their masters, to abstain from conquest and ensure economy. But their period of rule was not without trouble, both internal and external, and indeed it must have early become clear to any thinking observer of Indian affairs that England's sword would soon have to be drawn from its scabbard once more.

No sooner had the army marched back to its peace stations after the close of Lake's campaign against Holkar than it broke out into serious disaffection. The native troops in garrison at Vellore mutinied as a result of an injudicious change in their uniform, which was construed by them into an attack on their religion, and the movement was prevented from spreading only by the vigorous and timely intervention of Gillespie and his British dragoons from Arcot. Soon after the old question of reduction of the field allowance caused a renewed attempt at organised resistance among the commissioned ranks; the affair was not well handled by Minto, and sporadic outbreaks of disorder occurred in various places before a satisfactory settlement was arrived at.

Apart from these anxieties, the situation both within and without the territory nominally subject to the British was heavy with menace. The reduction of the Mahratta. armies forced upon the various chieftains of the confederacy by Lord Wellesley had let loose upon Central India a host of lawless and masterless men, who all their lives had subsisted by their swords, and now devoted themselves to preying on their peaceful neighbours. These men, formed into organised bands under elected leaders and known as Pindaris, soon became the terror of the countryside, and spread their ravages far and wide, burning, plundering, raping, destroying and creating a veritable reign of terror throughout the wide regions subjected to their depredations. Secretly or openly in league with these miscreants' were the various Mahratta chieftains, afraid for the present to tempt once more the fortune of open war against the powerful enemy who had so recently and so signally overwhelmed them and their armies, but only too eager to seize any chance of covertly discrediting British authority and undermining British prestige, and biding their time for revenge. Farther afield, beyond the frontiers of our territory, new and formidable states were arising, which might soon become our rivals or enemies. On the north the Gurkhas of Nepal, whose power had during the last half-century been spreading steadily westward, had extended their frontiers to the Sutlej, and were adopting a provocative policy of raids and incursions from the Himalayan foot-hills into British territory, of parts of which they in 1813 proceeded to take violent possession. Beyond that river, in the plains of the Punjab, Ranjit Singh was engaged in laying firm the foundations of an ominously powerful military state, with which in 1809 the British were within a hair's-breadth of becoming engaged in hostilities, while far to the north-west there was now arising for the first time that cloud which has ever since overhung that distant horizon—the possibility of a Russian invasion, which might at this time, in accordance with the terms of the Treaty of Tilsit, have the assistance of a French expeditionary corps. To this last menace Minto strove to oppose a coalition of barrier states—the Punjab, Sind, Afghanistan and Persia, with all of which he opened up friendly relations; while in the interior of India he exerted himself to keep the peace, at all events in his own time. In this, despite an occasional crisis such as that caused by the incursion of one of Holkar's lieutenants into Berar and the turbulence of a gang of minor chiefs in Bundelcund, he was on the whole successful, and if by reason of this policy he handed over to his successor, Lord Moira, whose earlier military achievements as Lord Rawdon in the War of American Independence we have already had occasion to notice, a heritage of thorny problems, he at least kept his military forces free to undertake those expeditions against the French and Dutch possessions in the East Indies which form a minor but highly creditable episode in the history of the Napoleonic Wars.

Moira, soon after his arrival at Calcutta in the autumn of 1813, realised that among the questions that most pressingly called for solution, that of the future relations between British India and Nepal was of primary importance. In April 1814 he therefore sent an ultimatum, calling for the instant evacuation of the lands recently occupied by the Gurkhas, and on the latter's refusal to comply, proceeded to enforce his demands by armed action. The military task to which he had set his hand promised to be no easy one, for his adversaries, though they could dispose of but 12,000 men, were a brave and wily race of hill men, fighting in a country well known to them, capable of rapid movement and skilled at the speedy erection of formidable stockades; while the British, whose troops were neither equipped nor trained for mountain warfare, would have to seek their foes in a region into which few white men had ever penetrated, and of which almost all that was known was that the difficulty of ensuring adequate transport and supply would be unprecedented.

A force of 34,000 men was assembled for the campaign and divided into four columns. Of these the two westernmost under Ochterlony and Gillespie, the hero of Vellore and Java, were to move north from their area of concentration between the upper Ganges and the Sutlej against the flanks and rear of the main Gurkha army, which was known to be on the left bank of the latter river west of Simla; a third from Benares was to cut the enemy line of communications with Katmandu, their capital, 100 miles west of that place, which was simultaneously to be attacked by the fourth column from Patna. This ambitious scheme of operations broke down from the very start; the two right-hand columns, timidly led, were sharply checked; Gillespie lost his life in an unsuccessful attack on a hill fort near Dehra Dun; and only Ochterlony, whose skilful operations stand out all the more strongly by reason of the ineptitude of his colleagues, pursued his advance against the Gurkha army, which he at length, after six months' methodical operations, brought to battle in a strong position at Malaon, and completely defeated. This success redeemed all our other failures, and Kumaon having meantime been overrun by another British force, the Gurkhas were reduced to asking for terms, which, however, on receiving they refused to accept. Accordingly operations were renewed; Ochterlony was placed in chief command of an army of 20,000 men, and moved from Patna direct on Katmandu; all the formidable enemy fortifications were one by one turned and abandoned to the invaders, who had reached a point within 30 miles of the capital when the Gurkhas once more, and this time in earnest, sued for peace, which was duly concluded in March 1816. By its terms the British gained an area of valuable territory to the west and south of Nepal, within which were to be situated the hill stations of the Government and the army—and later acquired, what was of still greater importance, the friendship of a gallant people who have since furnished the Indian army with some of its best regiments, and its most desirable recruits.

During the course of the Gurkha War another minor campaign had been taken in hand at the opposite extremity of India for the subjection of the native kingdom in the interior of Ceylon, which twelve years before had, as will be remembered, successfully repulsed invasion. Little effective resistance was now encountered by the various small columns, numbering some 4000 men in all, which converged upon Kandy from all sides in the spring of 1815; but various insurrectionary movements in the outlying districts kept the British troops, whose losses from disease were severe, fully occupied for some three years before the island could be said to be finally subdued.

No sooner had the dispute with Nepal been settled by force of arms than the Governor-General was compelled to turn his attention to the problem of Central India, where the activity of the Pindaris was growing from a scandal to a menace. In 1815 and again in the following year they made a number of serious incursions into British territory, carrying fire and sword southwards beyond the Kistna, and eastwards and westwards as far as the Carnatic coast, and the shores of the Indian Ocean south of Bombay. Accordingly Moira decided to take the field and put an end to the pest once for all, but his task was complicated by the necessity of simultaneously keeping a close watch on the Mahratta chiefs, who were with justice suspected of intriguing against the paramount power.

Whereas the Pindaris were estimated to number little more that 30,000 all told, and were known to be of little value as fighting men, the various Mahratta states could put into the field some 180,000 troops of all arms, whose military reputation was considerable. The Governor-General therefore assembled for the forthcoming campaign a mass of 113,000 men with over 300 guns— the largest British army yet seen in India. In the north the Grand Army, under his own personal command, 43,000 men in all, assembled on the line of the Ganges between Delhi and Allahabad, and was destined to advance from north and east on the Pindaris' line in Malwa, north of the Nerbudda, while the Army of the Deccan, numbering 70,000 men, under Sir Thomas Hislop, concentrating on the line of that river, from Hoshangabad to Gujerat, drove the enemy northwards into the arms of their comrades. Hislop's reserve divisions, posted in Khandesh, to the west of Berar, and in the north-west corner of Hyderabad, were to support the main advance and keep an eye on the Mahrattas, while a defensive cordon of posts, still farther to the south along the line of the Kistna from sea to sea, were to guard the frontier of British territory against any predatory bands which might escape the net drawn around them.

The preparations for these widespread operations were prolonged, largely by reason of unfavourable weather, throughout the whole of the spring and summer of 1817, and it was not till well on into November that all was ready for the combined advance. Then, at the moment assigned for its commencement, the grand scheme was disarranged by an outbreak of hostilities on the part of the Mahrattas in rear of the Army of the Deccan. Baji Rao, the Peshwa, and Apa Sahib, the Bhonsla, both suddenly assailed the British detachments guarding the Residencies at Poona and at Nagpur with overwhelming forces; both were heroically repulsed, but Hislop felt himself compelled to despatch a large proportion of his troops to deal with the rebels, and was only prevented by direct and precise orders from Moira from abandoning altogether the advance against the Pindaris. At the same time a serious epidemic of cholera devastated the ranks of the Grand Army, and the joint operations thus commenced under the most unfavourable auspices. None the less, they were executed according to programme and with satisfactory enough results. The first marches of Moira's divisions placed Sindia, whose artillery was collected in his capital at Gwalior while the remainder of his army was stationed far to the west and south-west of that city, in such a position that he had no choice but to conclude the treaty of alliance tendered him by the British, who thus disposed of one potential enemy. Shortly afterwards the advance of Hislop's columns, by driving the Pindaris back from the Nerbudda into the arms of Holkar's army north of Ujjein, compelled that prince also to show his hand; choosing to ally himself with the outlaws, he was brought to action at Mehidpur, and although his 35,000 men, strongly posted, far outnumbered the British, who fought their battle with more courage than skill, suffered complete defeat. The treaty concluded some weeks later inflicted on him as the price of his treachery the loss of all his territory south of the Nerbudda.

Meanwhile in the south the Peshwa had abandoned Poona on the approach of the British relieving columns and taken to the open country, while Apa Sahib had been overawed and reduced to abject submission, and was practically a state prisoner in his own capital. Thus the campaign both here and in the north resolved itself into the chase of an active and elusive but no longer formidable foe. Baji Rao, retreating rapidly first to the south and then to the east, outdistanced his pursuers, and, doubling back towards Poona, encountered a detachment of 500 sepoys under Staunton, who took refuge in the village of Koregaon, and held out for a day and a night against the repeated attacks of 28,000 enemies. This heroic feat blasted all the Peshwa's hopes of recovering his capital and left him no resource but renewed flight. For the next few weeks he moved rapidly to and fro between the Kistna and Godavery, until Moira, in February 1818, realising that continual direct pursuit of him would be a lengthy and profitless task, decided to entrust the chase to a number of light columns of mounted troops, and to bring him to terms by the reduction of his fortresses and the complete occupation of his country. Some days later, as luck would have it, one of these light columns encountered Baji Rao at Ashti and dispersed the greater part of his following, and in June he himself was rounded up near Asirgarh and compelled to capitulate unconditionally. He was deposed from his throne and became a pensioner of the British; but the occupation of his territory proceeded but slowly, and it was not till March 1819 that Asirgarh, the last of his fortresses to hold out, was battered into surrender.

The extermination of the Pindaris had all this time been proceeding methodically, and by February 1818 they were no longer a force to be seriously reckoned with, such as survived being reduced to a few skulking bands, too few in numbers and too cowed even to face the villagers upon whom they had formerly preyed. While these fugitive bodies were being hunted and exterminated by small mobile columns, the greater part of the British divisions were broken up, the units composing them returning to their peace stations. By the end of 1818 peace had been completely restored, and the few Pindari chiefs who survived the dispersal of their followers—including the Bhonsla Apa Sahib, who had escaped from his British captors but had been unable to collect any troops to help him to regain his throne—were living with a few companions the harried life of outlaws.

Thus the British had asserted beyond dispute their sway over Central India, and had added to the vast dominion already owning direct or indirect allegiance to them the wide expanse of territory formerly ruled by the Mahratta Confederacy. In truth the Mahratta troops had shown themselves, in this last war at any rate, as contemptible in battle as any that had ever fled before our arms, and Moira's main difficulty had been not to defeat them but to find an opportunity for doing so. Nonetheless, this task too—and how toilsome and thankless a task it is has been shown by the guerrilla warfare in South Africa, in 1899-1902, to which the campaign just described bears many points of resemblance—had been admirably accomplished, thanks mainly to the foresight, industry and painstaking thoroughness of the Governor-General, who, by his conduct of this campaign, proved himself well worthy to a place in history beside the greatest of our organisers of victory, Amherst and Kitchener. It is one of the ironies of fate that Moira's operations in 1817-1819, which are perhaps, for the lessons which may be learned from them and their applicability to the present day, better worth study than anything in our Indian military annals prior to the Mutiny, should, by reason of the very completeness of their success, and the absence of any dramatic achievement in battle, be an unknown chapter even to well-informed students and soldiers.

It will be convenient here to deal with two episodes which, though somewhat out of place as regards chronology, form a necessary epilogue to the story of the subjugation of Central India. Five years after the last of the Pindaris had been driven into the jungle, and when the military energies of British India were deeply involved, as we shall see, in a heart-breaking campaign in Burma, a disputed succession in Bhurtpore necessitated our armed intervention. To deal with this fortress, which had gained a somewhat fictitious reputation from Lake's repeated failures before its walls twenty years before, the Commander-in-Chief, Lord Combermere, assembled an army of 27,000 men, equipped with what Lake had lacked, an adequate siege train of over 100 guns. After less than a month's investment the place, though held by a garrison as strong or stronger than the besieging force, was stormed at little cost, and its defenders for all practical purposes exterminated or taken; and thus bloodily and effectively was British prestige, shaken by causes both remote and recent, restored to its former height.

The second episode took place nearly twenty years later, at a time when the military fame of Great Britain, after having once more fallen to a low ebb by reason of the serious disaster which had befallen the army in the First Afghan War, had been only partially restored by her successes in the latter part of that war and in Sind, while the political horizon was clouded by the critical state of her relations with the Sikhs of the Punjab. The house of Sindia, the only member of the Mahratta Confederacy who had not felt the weight of British arms in the field in 1817, owing to its enforced surrender to our demands, narrated above, now became embroiled with us by reason of a disputed succession to the throne in 1843, and the seizure of power by an anti-British candidate. Sindia's army, numbering 22,000 good troops, was a formidable menace which required to be instantly dealt with, and an equal British force was assembled in two bodies, the one under Sir H. Gough, the Commander-in-Chief, south-west of Agra, the other under Grey, near Jhansi, with orders to converge on Gwalior. The campaign, which lasted only forty-eight hours, was the briefest and one of the most decisive in our history. The Mahrattas, who fought unevenly, were hopelessly defeated in a double battle on the same day, by Gough at Maharajpore and by Grey at Punniar, though in the former engagement they outnumbered their adversaries by nearly two to one, and were compelled to accept the treaty imposed upon them, the main clause being the drastic reduction of their army and the incorporation into it of a contingent of British sepoy troops. During the Mutiny this contingent was destined to give us more trouble than the conquered Mahrattas, whose pretensions to ascendancy in Central India were finally shattered by the campaign of 1843 and who henceforward disappear from history as an independent power. With their overthrow was finally accomplished the third stage in the British conquest of India.

A Note on the Gwalior War

The Gwalior War

Gwalior and its territories were of significant strategic importance to British intentions in the sub-continent, but following setbacks for the British in Afghanistan and elsewhere, the ruling elite of Gwalior were determined to go their own way, and refused to give assurances that their significant military potential—a combined Maratha and Sikh force of around 120,000 men and 500 guns—would not be used against the British. The Gwalior Council of Regency refused to even contemplate an agreement with Lord Ellenborough, the then Governor-General, and, in 1843, war was declared.

The British East India Company army massed 12,000 troops and 40 light field-pieces at Agra under Sir Hugh Gough, and 4,000 troops, consisting of two cavalry and three infantry brigades, at Jansi under Major-General John Grey. Opposing them was the Gwalior force, which included European-trained "regulars" as well as native troops and a considerable force of artillery.

On 29th December, Grey's troops crossed the River Jumna at Calpee and encountered a Maratha force some 12,000 strong at Punniar. Grey ordered the attack, the Marathas were routed and much artillery was captured. Some 20 miles away Gough's forces battled about 17,000 Marathas in a strong position at Maharajpoor. Naturally Gough attacked immediately and, despite strong resistance, the Marathas were routed and 56 guns captured. Gough suffered almost 800 casualties.

In his book Colonial Small Wars, military historian Donald Featherstone says:

> With two small British armies converging from opposite directions and acting quite independently of each other, the Mahrattas should have concentrated their forces and attacked either in detail, but they neglected this opportunity ....

The Gwalior War is one of the British *small wars* of the Victorian era that has been little written about; certainly contemporary (or near contemporary) accounts—whether first-hand or historical—of this brief episode in the history of Britain, India and the Honourable East India Company are hard to come by, but we offer here two short pieces that we hope will add some detail to the brief outline we have given above.

The account that follows is from a letter written by Sir Harry Smith to Sir James Kempt, dated Gwalior, 15th January, 1844.

Sir Harry Smith on the Battle of Maharajpore

The army did march as described in Sir H. Gough's dispatches in three columns, each arriving at its designated post in excellent time—which I freely admit was scarcely to be expected, having to disengage itself from a mass of laden elephants, camels, and bullocks and bullock carts, etc., resembling rather the multitudes of Xerxes than anything modern, and having to traverse ground on the banks of rivulets most peculiarly intersected by numerous and deep small ravines, the pigmy model of a chain of mountains, but even more impassable. On such ravines was posted the enemy's left flank; his right extended towards the village of Maharajpore, which he had filled with Infantry and ably supported by batteries enfilading its approach, his extreme right again thrown back upon the ravines of the Ahsin River, as described in the little pencil sketch enclosed, thus realizing the surmise in my report, 'his right *"en air,"* as if other troops were coming up to complete the occupation of the position.'

If we could have caught the enemy in the state he was when reconnoitred the previous day, easy indeed would have been the victory.

These Mahrattas, nor indeed does any Indian Army, know no more than to occupy a strong position and hold it as long as able, sticking to their guns like men. Having observed the enemy's position the day before, it was obvious to me this morning that he had advanced very considerably, and that he held the village of Maharajpore in force, which I rode through the day previous. Upon a plain, and that plain covered with the high stalks of Jumna corn, not a mound of rising ground even to assist the view, reconnoitring is nearly nominal. However, so impressed was I from what a nearer view the day before had given me and what I then saw, that the enemy attached great importance to his left flank, the line of his retreat if beaten, I ventured to advocate that flank as the most eligible point for a weighty attack.

However, things were differently conducted and as the heads of columns appeared, the enemy instantly opened a well-directed cannonade, particularly from the vicinity of the village of Maharajpore, and Sir H.

Gough ordered an advance. His dispatch tells the tale, and the mode of resistance, the enemy's guns, etc. I need, therefore, only bear testimony to the gallantry of the enemy's resistance, which in my conscience I believe and assert would not have been overcome but for our gallant old Peninsular comrades, the 39th and 40th Regiments, who carried everything before them, bayoneting the gunners at their guns to a man. These guns were most ably posted, each battery flanking and supporting the other by as heavy a cross-fire of cannon as I ever saw, and grape like hail. Our leaders of brigades in the neighbourhood and in the village had various opportunities of displaying heroism, Valiant, Wright 39th and my Assistant, Major Barr, remarkably so, and many gallant fellows fell in this noble performance of their duty.

The enemy was driven back at every point with great loss, yielding to force, not retiring in haste. A more thorough devotedness to their cause no soldiers could evince, and the annals of their defeat, altho' an honour to us, can never be recorded as any disgrace to them. Turn we now to General Grey's division. For many days before the 29th our communication was totally interrupted, and the wisdom of the route and the disunited approach to Gwalior must be tested by the fortunate result, not by the established rules and principles of strategy. Grey's dispatch is not so well written as it might have been, I am led to understand, nor does he give full credit to the old Buffs for their gallant double allowance with which they contributed to the achievements of the day and the capture of the enemy's guns, every one of them.

The old 50th had its share too, and the blockheads in the East, who 'haver' over their wine of India's being in a state to require no British troops, are wrong: for, liberally contributing the full meed of praise to the Sepoy Battalions, that praise is so rested on the British soldier's example, the want of that *'point d'appui'* would entail a dire want indeed, that of victory! Now if we regard the victories recently obtained over the Mahratta force, 28,000 men whose discipline has gradually been improving under Christian officers since 1803 (the days of Lake and Wellington), well supplied with cannon and every implement of war, animated by a devotion to their cause not to be exceeded–in a military point of view they are achievements in the field which yield alone to Assaye and rank with Dieg, Laswarree, and Mehudpore, and in a political point of view, their importance is immense, struck in the very heart of India, within the hearing almost of the seat of government of our Upper Provinces, Agra.

Remembering the disasters in Afghanistan, which still, as they ever will, hold their baneful influence over British India; reviewing the recent bloody murders, and present confusion and anarchy at Lahore; the still unsettled state of Bundelkund; the sickness in Scinde (that accursed Scinde), the grave of our army; the intrigues at the court of Nepal, which have been rife and ready for mischief pending the late contest—then may my Lord Ellenborough and our country congratulate themselves upon the re-establishment of the 'Prestige of our Arms' as a sure foundation of our Indian Empire, the very base of which was tremulous, for it is well known that these Mahrattas have been advocating hostility in every court of the East.

It is to be hoped, therefore, coupled with Lord E.'s moderation and the equity of his acts in thus re-establishing the youthful Maharaja on his throne, that our country and its Government will regard this as no war of foreign invasion, no war of conquest and unjust aggression, but one of absolute necessity to maintain the one Power paramount in India on the faith of old treaties of amity, and a demonstration to the present disturbed states of India, to the well-disposed, and to the World, that the British Lion will be ever triumphant; and that it will accordingly treat the soldiers who have achieved victories of such political magnitude with the liberality shown to the heroes exiled from Afghanistan, their discomfitures conjured into triumphs of valour, their miserable retreat through the Khyber Pass into deeds of glory inferior to none but the passage of San Bernardo by Napoleon. In this hope we may venture to trust a fair construction will be put on our acts, and that I may see my gallant comrades promoted as they deserve, and honoured in the manner recent services have been.

I shall ever regard this battle as one of the most fortunate circumstances of my life, if the majority of its remainder is to be spent in India, by its having acquired me that experience in Indian warfare all require, and above all, to hold in just estimation your enemy, a creed I have ever advocated, and to a certain extent, in every instance practised. In the late conflict no one gave our foe credit for half his daring or ability; hence our attack was not quite so scientifically powerful by a combination of the different arms as it might have been, and the defects of the unwieldy machine called the British Indian Army rendered most glaring:—its appalling quantity of baggage, its lack of organization and equipment of the soldiers, its want of experience in Generals and in officers, the extreme willingness but total inexpertness and inaptitude of the soldier in the arts of war, in the conflict, on picquet, on every duty which a protracted campaign alone can teach effectually.

In this country almost every war has been terminated in one or two pitched battles fought so soon as the one army comes in sight of the other, and accordingly all the science attaching to advance and retreat, the posting of picquets, reconnaissance of the enemy, the daily contemplating his movements, both when he is before you and on the march, are lost, and war is reduced at once to 'there are people drawn up who will shoot at you, so fire away at them.' You blindly and ineptly rush upon them, drive them from the field with considerable loss, take all their guns, and never see the vestige of them after. Thus we must judiciously and with foresight organize ourselves for a campaign in the Punjab—a very probable event—for the armies of India are not now the rabble they were in Clive's time, but organized and disciplined by European officers of experience (many French), and the art of war has progressed rapidly among our enemies, whose troops are invariably far more numerous than those we oppose to them; thus by superior ability we could alone calculate on their defeat. As it is, we calculate alone on the bulldog courage of Her Majesty's soldiers, and our loss becomes what we lately witnessed.

To obviate these deficiencies, apparent even to the most inexperienced eye, we must in the first place reduce our baggage, next give our Sepoys canteens and haversacks (a Regiment told me they were exhausted for want of water, the water-carriers having run away). We must then, every cold season, have divisions of the army assembled, and post the one half opposite the other, with outlying picquets, etc., and daily alarms, skirmishes, etc., then general actions with blank cartridges. Without this the British Indian Army will remain as it now is—a great unwieldy machine of ignorant officers and soldiers. The drill of the Sepoy is good enough, and that of his officer, and never will attain greater perfection, but unless the officers in their separate commands know how, as I call it, to feed the fight, to bring up or into action successively in their places their command, when the attack is ordered, I defy any general to defeat his enemy but by stupid bull-dog courage. It may be conceit in Harry Smith, but if 10,000 men were given him in one cold season, if by sham fights, etc., he did not make them practical soldiers, he would resign in disgust, for the material is excellent and willing, but now, like a dictionary, it contains all the words, but cannot write a letter.

We go now from an eye-witness report to an historical account borrowed from the book *Our Soldiers* by W. H. G. Kingston (1899). Ostensibly written for teenagers the account is nonetheless valuable for being one of the few written at a time when participants in the Gwalior War may still have been alive.

The Gwalior Campaign, 1843
Battle of Maharajpoor

The loss of British prestige in the defiles of Afghanistan had induced many of the native princes of India to fancy that the power of England was on the wane, and that they might assume a tone of authority and independence which they would not before have ventured to exhibit. Among others, the Maratha Court at Gwalior adopted a line of policy inimical to British interests, and contrary to the engagements into which their princes had entered.

Lord Ellenborough, foreseeing that they would make an attempt to emancipate themselves altogether from British influence, assembled an army on the frontier facing the Maratha territory, and called it the "Army of Exercise." It was gradually increased, and placed under the command of Sir Hugh Gough. Various insulting acts having been committed by the Maratha Government against the English, and no apology having been made, the Governor-General ordered the army to enter the Maratha territory.

General Grey took the lead with a division of infantry and a brigade of cavalry, and, crossing the Jumna at Calpee, threatened the Gwalior territory from the south; while two divisions of infantry, and two brigades of cavalry, with the usual complement of artillery, moved down from the northward under the command of Sir Hugh Gough himself. General Grey, having advanced from Bundelcund, reached Panniar, about 12 miles from Gwalior, on the 28th of December. The enemy, estimated at about 12,000 in number, took up a strong position on the heights near the fortified village of Mangore. Although the British troops were much fatigued by their long march, the enemy were immediately attacked and driven from height to height, till the rout was completed. The British loss was 215 killed and wounded.

Sir Hugh Gough advanced, and found the enemy awaiting him at a strong post which they had selected on the evening of the 28th. It was reconnoitred; but during the night the Maratha forces left their entrenched position, and took up another three or four miles in advance of it. The British troops numbered about 14,000 men, with 40 pieces of artillery. The Mahrattas mustered 18,000 men, including 3000 cavalry and 100 guns. The Maratha army had under Scindia been carefully organised by European officers, and was therefore composed of well-disciplined men, equal in bravery to any of the natives of India.

On the morning of the 29th, no fresh reconnaissance having been made, the British forces found themselves in the presence of an enemy they fancied some miles off. Many ladies, on their elephants, were on the field when the action commenced by the gallant advance of Major-General Littler's column upon the enemy, in front of the village of Maharajpoor.

The enemy's guns committed severe execution as they advanced; and though the Mahrattas fought with the most desperate courage, nothing could withstand the headlong rush of the British soldiers. Her Majesty's 39th Foot, with their accustomed dash, ably supported by the 56th Native Infantry, drove the enemy from their guns into the village, bayoneting the gunners at their posts. Here a sanguinary conflict took place. The fierce Mahrattas, after discharging their matchlocks, fought sword in hand with the most determined courage. General Valiant's brigade, with equal enthusiasm, took Maharajpoor in reverse, and 28 guns were captured by this combined movement. So desperately did the defenders of this strong position fight, that few escaped. During these operations, Brigadier Scott was opposed by a body of the enemy's cavalry on the extreme left, and made some well-executed charges with the 10th Light Cavalry, most ably supported by Captain Grant's troop of horse artillery, and the 4th Lancers, capturing some guns and taking two standards, thus threatening the right flank of the enemy.

On this, as on every occasion, Sir Henry, then Captain Havelock, distinguished himself. The 56th Native Infantry, who had been brigaded with Her Majesty's 39th, were advancing on the enemy, but at so slow a pace as to exhaust the patience of Sir Hugh Gough.

"Will no one get that sepoy regiment on?" he exclaimed.

Havelock offered to go, and riding up, inquired the name of the corps.

"It is the 56th Native Infantry."

"I don't want its number," replied he. "What is its native name?"

"*Lamboorunke pultum*—Lambourn's regiment."

He then took off his cap, and placing himself in their front, addressed them by that name, and in a few complimentary and cheering words reminded them that they fought under the eye of the Commander-in-Chief. He then led them up to the batteries, and afterwards remarked, that "whereas it had been difficult to get them forward before, the difficulty now was to restrain their impetuosity."

In conformity with the previous instructions, Major-general Valiant, supported by the 3rd Cavalry Brigade, moved on the right of the enemy's position at Chouda. During the advance he had to take in succession three strongly entrenched positions, where the enemy defended their guns with frantic desperation. Here Her Majesty's 40th Regiment lost two successive commanding officers, Major Stopford and Captain Coddington, who fell wounded at the very muzzles of the guns. It captured four regimental standards. This corps was ably and nobly supported by the 2nd and 16th Grenadiers, under Lieutenant-Colonels Hamilton and McLarey. Major—General Littler, with Brigadier Wright's brigade, after dispersing the right of the enemy's position at Maharajpoor, steadily advanced to fulfil his instructions to attack the main position at Chouda, and was supported most ably by Captain Grant's troop of horse artillery, and the 1st Regiment of Light Cavalry. This column had to advance under a severe fire, over very difficult ground, but when within a short distance of the enemy, the gallant 39th Regiment, as before, rushing forward, led by Major Bray, and gallantly supported by the 56th Regiment, under Major Dick, carried everything before them, and thus gained the entrenched main position of Chouda.

The battle of Maharajpoor was now virtually won. The loss on both sides had been severe. The British had 106 killed, of whom 7 were officers, and 684 wounded, and 7 missing, making a total loss of 797. The Mahrattas are supposed to have lost between 3000 and 4000 men.

In consequence of this victory and that of Panniar, the Maratha Durbar submitted to the British Government. Lieutenant-Colonel Stubbs was appointed governor of the fort of Gwalior, which commands the city. The Maratha troops were disbanded, and a British contingent was formed, to be maintained at the cost of the Gwalior Government, which was compelled to pay forthwith the expenses of the campaign.

The observant will have noticed that the figures given for the strength of the opposing armies in the above account differ somewhat from the now widely accepted figures quoted earlier. It is Leonaur policy to change as little as possible in the accounts we publish, so these have been left unchanged.

The Leonaur Editors

ALSO FROM LEONAUR
AVAILABLE IN SOFTCOVER OR HARDCOVER WITH DUST JACKET

SEPOYS, SIEGE & STORM *by Charles John Griffiths*—The Experiences of a young officer of H.M.'s 61st Regiment at Ferozepore, Delhi ridge and at the fall of Delhi during the Indian mutiny 1857.

CAMPAIGNING IN ZULULAND *by W. E. Montague*—Experiences on campaign during the Zulu war of 1879 with the 94th Regiment.

THE STORY OF THE GUIDES *by G. J. Younghusband*—The Exploits of the Soldiers of the famous Indian Army Regiment from the northwest frontier 1847 - 1900..

ZULU: 1879 *by D.C.F. Moodie & the Leonaur Editors*—The Anglo-Zulu War of 1879 from contemporary sources: First Hand Accounts, Interviews, Dispatches, Official Documents & Newspaper Reports.

THE RECOLLECTIONS OF SKINNER OF SKINNER'S HORSE *by James Skinner*—James Skinner and his 'Yellow Boys' Irregular cavalry in the wars of India between the British, Mahratta, Rajput, Mogul, Sikh & Pindarree Forces.

TOMMY ATKINS' WAR STORIES 14 FIRST HAND ACCOUNTS—Fourteen first hand accounts from the ranks of the British Army during Queen Victoria's Empire Original & True Battle Stories Recollections of the Indian Mutiny With the 49th in the Crimea With the Guards in Egypt The Charge of the Six Hundred With Wolseley in Ashanti Alma, Inkermann and Magdala With the Gunners at Tel-el-Kebir Russian Guns and Indian Rebels Rough Work in the Crimea In the Maori Rising Facing the Zulus From Sebastopol to Lucknow Sent to Save Gordon On the March to Chitral Tommy by Rudyard Kipling

CHASSEUR OF 1914 *by Marcel Dupont*—Experiences of the twilight of the French Light Cavalry by a young officer during the early battles of the great war in Europe.

TROOP HORSE & TRENCH *by R. A. Lloyd*—The experiences of a British Lifeguardsman of the household cavalry fighting on the western front during the First World War 1914-18.

THE EAST AFRICAN MOUNTED RIFLES *by C. J. Wilson*—Experiences of the campaign in the East African bush during the First World War.

THE FIGHTING CAMELIERS *by Frank Reid*—The exploits of the Imperial Camel Corps in the desert and Palestine campaigns of the First World War.

AVAILABLE ONLINE AT
www.leonaur.com
AND OTHER GOOD BOOK STORES

ALSO FROM LEONAUR
AVAILABLE IN SOFTCOVER OR HARDCOVER WITH DUST JACKET

THE COMPLEAT RIFLEMAN HARRIS *by Benjamin Harris as told to & transcribed by Captain Henry Curling*—The adventures of a soldier of the 95th (Rifles) during the Peninsular Campaign of the Napoleonic Wars

WITH WELLINGTON'S LIGHT CAVALRY *by William Tomkinson*—The Experiences of an officer of the 16th Light Dragoons in the Peninsular and Waterloo campaigns of the Napoleonic Wars.

SERGEANT BOURGOGNE *by Adrien Bourgogne*—With Napoleon's Imperial Guard in the Russian Campaign and on the Retreat from Moscow 1812 - 13.

SWORDS OF HONOUR *by Henry Newbolt & Stanley L. Wood*—The Careers of Six Outstanding Officers from the Napoleonic Wars, the Wars for India and the American Civil War, with dozens of illustrations by Stanley L. Wood.

SURTEES OF THE RIFLES *by William Surtees*—A Soldier of the 95th (Rifles) in the Peninsular campaign of the Napoleonic Wars.

ENSIGN BELL IN THE PENINSULAR WAR *by George Bell*—The Experiences of a young British Soldier of the 34th Regiment 'The Cumberland Gentlemen' in the Napoleonic wars.

HUSSAR IN WINTER *by Alexander Gordon*—A British Cavalry Officer during the retreat to Corunna in the Peninsular campaign of the Napoleonic Wars.

NAPOLEONIC WAR STORIES *by Sir Arthur Quiller-Couch*—Tales of soldiers, spies, battles & sieges from the Peninsular & Waterloo campaingns.

JOURNALS OF ROBERT ROGERS OF THE RANGERS *by Robert Rogers*—The exploits of Rogers & the Rangers in his own words during 1755-1761 in the French & Indian War.

KERSHAW'S BRIGADE VOLUME 1 *by D. Augustus Dickert*—Manassas, Seven Pines, Sharpsburg (Antietam), Fredricksburg, Chancellorsville, Gettysburg, Chickamauga, Chattanooga, Fort Sanders & Bean Station..

KERSHAW'S BRIGADE VOLUME 2 *by D. Augustus Dickert*—At the wilderness, Cold Harbour, Petersburg, The Shenandoah Valley and Cedar Creek.

A TIGER ON HORSEBACK *by L. March Phillips*—The Experiences of a Trooper & Officer of Rimington's Guides - The Tigers - during the Anglo-Boer war 1899 - 1902.

AVAILABLE ONLINE AT
www.leonaur.com
AND OTHER GOOD BOOK STORES

ALSO FROM LEONAUR
AVAILABLE IN SOFTCOVER OR HARDCOVER WITH DUST JACKET

CAPTAIN OF THE 95th (Rifles) *by Jonathan Leach*—An officer of Wellington's Sharpshooters during the Peninsular, South of France and Waterloo Campaigns of the Napoleonic Wars.

THE KHAKEE RESSALAH *by Robert Henry Wallace Dunlop*—Service & adventure with the Meerut volunteer horse during the Indian mutiny 1857-1858

BUGLER AND OFFICER OF THE RIFLES *by William Green & Harry Smith* With the 95th (Rifles) during the Peninsular & Waterloo Campaigns of the Napoleonic Wars

BAYONETS, BUGLES AND BONNETS *by James 'Thomas' Todd*—Experiences of hard soldiering with the 71st Foot - the Highland Light Infantry - through many battles of the Napoleonic wars including the Peninsular & Waterloo Campaigns

A NORFOLK SOLDIER IN THE FIRST SIKH WAR *by J W Baldwin*—Experiences of a private of H.M. 9th Regiment of Foot in the battles for the Punjab, India 1845-46

A CAVALRY OFFICER DURING THE SEPOY REVOLT *by A.R.D. Mackenzie*—Experiences with the 3rd Bengal Light Cavalry, the Guides and Sikh Irregular Cavalry from the outbreak to Delhi and Lucknow

THE ADVENTURES OF A LIGHT DRAGOON *by George Farmer & G.R. Gleig*—A cavalryman during the Peninsular & Waterloo Campaigns, in captivity & at the siege of Bhurtpore, India

THE COMPLEAT RIFLEMAN HARRIS *by Benjamin Harris as told to & transcribed by Captain Henry Curling*—The adventures of a soldier of the 95th (Rifles) during the Peninsular Campaign of the Napoleonic Wars

THE RED DRAGOON *by W.J. Adams*—With the 7th Dragoon Guards in the Cape of Good Hope against the Boers & the Kaffir tribes during the 'war of the axe' 1843-48

THE LIFE OF THE REAL BRIGADIER GERARD - Volume 1 - THE YOUNG HUSSAR 1782 - 1807 *by Jean-Baptiste De Marbot*—A French Cavalryman Of the Napoleonic Wars at Marengo, Austerlitz, Jena, Eylau & Friedland

THE LIFE OF THE REAL BRIGADIER GERARD Volume 2 IMPERIAL AIDE-DE-CAMP 1807 - 1811 *by Jean-Baptiste De Marbot*—A French Cavalryman of the Napoleonic Wars at Saragossa, Landshut, Eckmuhl, Ratisbon, Aspern-Essling, Wagram, Busaco & Torres Vedras

AVAILABLE ONLINE AT
www.leonaur.com
AND OTHER GOOD BOOK STORES

www.ingramcontent.com/pod-product-compliance
Lightning Source LLC
Chambersburg PA
CBHW020949230426
43666CB00005B/240